Love Embodies the Truth

Works of love to be accomplished

All Scripture quotations, unless otherwise indicated,
are taken from the Holy Bible, English Standard Version.

This book introduces the author's lifelong journey of faith
along with quotations from Søren Kierkegaard's *Works of Love*
(New Jersey: Princeton University Press, 1995).

Love Embodies the Truth

Works of love to be accomplished

Munjung Ha

Editors

Jayong Kim

Roger and Janet Samra

HISWAY

Contents

Prologue

Various religions each have their respective gods. However, it is difficult to know exactly who the God of Christianity is among these gods. The Bible tells us that God revealed Himself through the incarnate Son of God. Through the *Works of Love*, Kierkegaard has approached the Christian God from an existential perspective. Kierkegaard's portrayal of God is through the lens of love which is a communicable attribute of God, a distinction from the usual approach of abstract concepts such as theory or knowledge. He describes that as man chooses to act in love and live by love, every moment that would normally end in vain becomes eternal. Moreover, by choosing love by the act of giving everything, he will gain God who is all in all although he might lose everything in this world.

We cannot find God in human religiosity because religion is man-made and man is not the truth. We know God, the Creator only through our life in which we can choose to accomplish the love of the truth. Love without the truth cannot reveal God to us. Love without the truth cannot overcome impurity. Love without the truth falls into self-satisfaction. However, love of the truth molds man into the fullness of Christ as he submits to the truth. Here the difference between human love and love of the truth is stark. Human love ultimately seeks only self-satisfaction, while in the eternal perspective that God has, self-satisfaction in love results in losing everything. Only love that goes along with the truth leads man to self-denial and ultimately gaining the eternal God.

Kierkegaard has successfully explained the great themes of Christianity including Jesus as the truth, the original sin of man, and the ultimate purpose of salvation with a single word, "love." With this word, he also explains the character of God such as God's righteousness and holiness. To achieve the ultimate, desired result of man's true salvation and union with God, Kierkegaard asserts that man must do "works of love" which are man's works done in absolute obedience to the absolute authority of the Word of God.

In these dark times when the light of the truth is fading with the Word losing its value and relativity gaining ground, the claim of Kierkegaard, which emphasizes man's absolute submission to God's absolute authority, is an astonishing teaching that shines like a star in the night sky. It is hard to find a person who knows the clarity of the truth that Kierkegaard saw because there are few people who have been as faithfully obedient to God as Kierkegaard was.

While walking the way of the cross, it is common for people to doubt or disbelieve whether we can discover the truth at the end of this path. Kierkegaard, however, persuades us from the top of the mountain of truth to abandon the temptations of inner darkness and self-love, and to instead obey God's command by faith. He was the one who accepted this absolute command as a great invitation and experienced how great God is to one such as him who received the invitation with sincere and true obedience.

At first, I started this book, *Love Embodies the Truth* for the purpose of introducing and sharing Kierkegaard's *Works of Love*, but as I continued writing and examining how God led me, I saw so many parallels between Kierkegaard's journey and mine that our path was one and the same. In this book, I would like to express my sincere respect for Kierkegaard, the great defender of the truth. As a great mentor, Kierkegaard encouraged me to go up to the mountain of the truth. I would also like to give my deepest gratitude to God for taking me to the truth, and also to Kierkegaard for shedding light on the way I walked by discovering this path as the vanguard. I sincerely hope that people who have doubts about the love of the truth will be challenged by the greatness of God's love through this book.

Chapter 1

Love is eternal

As we look not to the things that are seen but to the things that are unseen. For the things that are seen are transient, but the things that are unseen are eternal. (2 Cor. 4:18)

What is seen was not made out of things that are visible. (Heb. 11:3)

The Bible says that faith, hope, and love are eternal. How can faith, hope, and love exist forever? Man is finite. Thus, we cannot know whether faith, hope, and love are eternal. We know that faith, hope, and love do not belong to man. Man can invent or devise knowledge, philosophy, and religion. But we cannot conceive or envision faith, hope, and love. They do not belong to finite man, but to God. How can we know that these invisible values exist?

God is the object of faith and hope whereas man is not. We can hope for everything by believing in God. Faith and hope are gained only through God. Meanwhile, love is a communicable attribute that God and man have in common. Of course, the difference is obvious. God's love is eternal and unchanging while man's love is finite and changing. Humans, however, are the only ones that can transform finite and changing into eternal and unchanging love through their relationship with God. It is love with which eternity can be realized in human life. Human love overcomes despair through faith in God and is perfected in eternity.

Then how is this love fulfilled? The relationship between man and the Creator begins with man's obedience to the Word of the Creator. Through the Word, we come to believe that God is love and His love is eternal. Love and God are not separate. If man leaps to eternity in order to overcome the futility of life, it is equal to leaping to eternal love. To obtain eternity is to love and to love is to obey God's Word. Those who do not believe in eternity, however, do not make a leap to eternal love because they do not believe in God.

What do people choose when they do not choose eternal love? Ironically, they choose self-love, which does not have the eternal nature. But self-love, imperfect though it is, is still a sign that love exists and also a clue that makes some men wise enough to leap to eternity. People love themselves in the wrong way by not loving God while they focus on the present moment because they do not believe in eternity.

The important thing is that love exists in human life. Could there be anyone who does not love anything? In either direction (whether it is eternal love or self-love) when love ceases, man does not act. If love ceases, man dies. If you do not love God, you die for eternity and if you do not love yourself, the self dies. A man who loves God gains eternal life, while a man who loves himself without God gets an idol. God exists eternally as the essence of love, but man is connected to the love of truth only through being tied to eternal love. The will and mind of God who is the essential love are founded on love. But man who is not love in its essence can only gain the love of truth by yielding his will to eternal love through obedience.

Love is eternal and only by love is its eternity realized in this world. Why is it that we do not believe in true love? It is because we do not believe in God and eternity. This is why love is distorted. A man who does not believe in eternity cannot give eternal love which is accomplished and actualized only in eternal time. Love that lacks eternity loses its authenticity due to efforts to visualize love. When love is visible, it means that the love has already stopped in the moment. But love of eternity is genuine because of its eternal nature. In eternity, temporary human values and the love connected with them will disappear exposing their limits. Human love loses its power before eternal love. Indeed, human love in the face of eternal love comes to an end in a mere second.

Chapter 2

Love is the command

Beloved, let us love one another, for love is from God, and whoever loves has been born of God and knows God. Anyone who does not love does not know God, because God is love. (1 Jn. 4:7-8)

If you want to get the greatest love in this world, you must love God first. Man's love for God means a finite being's leap to the realm of eternity. Because God is love and His love is eternal, man gains eternal life only by loving the eternal God.

There is only one whom a person can with the truth of eternity love more than himself—that is God. Therefore it does not say, "You shall love God as yourself" but says, "You shall love the Lord your God with all your heart and all your soul and all your mind." A person should love God unconditionally *in obedience* and love him *in adoration*.[1]

Loving God is a way of overcoming human finitude. God has commanded us to love Him with all our heart, our will, and our sincerity. Man is inherently unable to give unchanging love to another man with all his heart, soul, and mind. A character with which we can give consistent love is built by our continuous obedience to the command of love. We are sometimes overwhelmed by the command to love God with all our heart, our will, and our sincerity. This is because we never had a purpose that required such an overwhelming passion and effort. There has to be a value worthy of pouring such passion to move man's heart, will, and mind.

You cannot invest eternity to get finitude. In order to gain eternity, however, we must invest something finite and ephemeral, which belongs to earthly life. It is not necessary to pour out your heart, will, and mind for the things that will change and disappear. However, it

1 Søren Kierkegaard, *Works of love* (New Jersey: Princeton University Press, 1995), 19.

will be a sure investment when you consume your heart, will, and mind for things that are unchanging and last forever. We will earn eternity only by a genuine motive that is formed when we do things with all our heart, will, and mind.

The commandment to "love God" is given to us by command. Mortal man, by nature, does not have any connection with God who is eternal. First, for mortal man to leap into eternity, he has to have a focused, sustained, and sincere desire for God. Through the command of love, we achieve this concentration and continuity. We can think of loving God as follows. For man, loving God means continuously choosing eternity. Choosing eternity is also equal to steadily discarding what is not eternity. That is, we cannot sincerely claim to love God with changing emotions, benevolent circumstances, or our preferences. The things that change do not belong to God. We must love what we do not have. And it is eternity. Therefore, to love God is to acquire eternity that we do not have. The commandment to "love God" is rather the way to "abandon the moment that fleetingly vanishes in vain and choose the unchanging and perpetual eternity."

Wherever the purely human wants to storm forth, the commandment constrains; wherever the purely human loses courage, the commandment strengthens; wherever the purely human becomes tired and sagacious, the commandment inflames and gives wisdom. The commandment consumes and burns out the unhealthiness in your love, but through the commandment you will in turn be able to rekindle it when it, humanly speaking, would cease.[2]

When we understand love from the eternal perspective, we understand why love as the command is just and fair. Furthermore, we now view the command as a kind and generous recommendation. The commandment to "love God" changes to "choose eternity." The imperative phrase "choose eternity" awakens us to our finite existence and tells us how wise it is to choose eternity considering human existence.

We now understand that we are able to love God only when we obey the command to love. If love is a choice, not a command, love

---

2 Ibid., 43.

becomes a dependent action, not a free choice. The reason for this is as follows. If love does not begin by a command, love will stop either until our unreliable emotions are ready for love, or until man is dissatisfied or skeptical about his existence and finally gives up his natural and nearly irresistible tendency to self-love. If love depends on the changeability of man, then such love is not strong enough to gain eternity.

We are bound to leap toward God and eternity through love. Love, therefore, must come to us as an active power that awakens us with the commandment to come out from the temporal and encourages us to do our best with our heart, will, and mind. Therefore, only love as the command gives us the utmost outcome.

You do not have the right to become insensitive to this feeling, because you *shall* love; but neither do you have the right to love despairingly, because you *shall* love, and just as little do you have the right to warp this feeling in you, because you *shall* love. You shall preserve love, and you shall preserve yourself and by and in preserving yourself preserve love.[3]

3 Ibid., 43.

Chapter 3

Love your neighbor

Christians choose love to gain eternal life. Loving is the way to approach the knowledge of God and Jesus Christ based on the following Word, "And this is eternal life, that they know you, the only true God, and Jesus Christ whom you have sent" (Jn. 17: 3). The problem is we do not know the love that leads to eternal life since man's love is self-love. In order for man to be free from self-gratifying love, he must start by loving a neighbor who is completely unrelated to his preference, not a preferential object of choice on a self-fulfilling basis. In other words, loving a neighbor who has nothing to do with my interest is the only way to discern whether the motivation to love is pure. Then, what can be the motive of love? It is to gain God and eternity by love. By loving a neighbor who is unrelated to one's preferences, human love is endowed with eternity, through which we gain God.[4]

> Christianity has thrust erotic love and friendship from the throne, the love based on drives and inclination, preferential love, in order to place the spirit's love [*Kjerlighed*] in its stead, love for the neighbor, a love that in earnestness and truth is more tender in inwardness than erotic love in the union and more faithful in sincerity than the most celebrated friendship in the alliance.[5]

How can we describe purely human love? Human love begins with preference and ends with satisfaction. Such love cannot have the eternal nature. Man constantly searches for objects of love in

---

4 To gain God means being closer to the presence of God, experiencing God, and coming to know God.

5 Ibid., 44.

order to obtain self-satisfaction or to satisfy his needs. The most fatal weakness of this love is that "it changes." This changeable nature of both subject (meaning the subject's preference or his/her volatile condition) and object of love leads to love that changes. Because of this capricious love, our object of preference has to also change. If a person says that his love has been unchanged, it can be said that he has possessive love. The stronger the passion for possession, the stronger the will one exerts. The downside of our love is the fact that "love changes" and that the moral obligation is softened as possessive love tends to restrain the loved one's freedom.

> To love without passion is an impossibility. But therefore the difference between erotic love and Christian love is also the only possible eternal difference in passion.[6]

Basically, preferential love does not like obligations. As for man's love, moral obligation becomes a shackle. As long as you choose

---

6 Ibid., 50.

obligation, your preference will lose its power. Preferential love cannot go with the command to love. The command to "love your neighbors," however, can be achieved only by obedience regardless of your preferences. The value of preferential love fades because this love hardly coexists with moral obligations. If love changes according to preferences, how precarious is this love? In order to maintain such love, we will have to make an effort to keep that particular condition. Love that is sustained through the continuous efforts of loved ones can only exist for the satisfaction of the lover. As a result, human love hardly goes beyond self-gratifying motivation.

For love to continue, moral obligation should not completely be removed. This obligation serves as a safeguard that keeps the relationship intact. Excluding moral obligation when giving love, which is the highest value human beings can pursue, contradicts itself. Morality is the most basic obligation for man, and if it is the highest value, man will voluntarily pursue it even beyond moral obligations. Therefore, it can be concluded that the value of genuine love fades because preferential love is not safe and can even vanish in the face of moral obligations.

When love excludes moral obligations, the subject of love has to be the absolute good. As the absolute good exists above moral obligations, it is not required of such obligations. Thus, preferential love is possible only when man excludes God and regards himself as the absolute good. Man is free from all moral obligations only when he denies God's order and considers his judgment as absolutely right. In this regard, preferential love is fleeting love that, from its inception, has nothing to do with eternity.

Moreover, just as self-love in the strictest sense has been designated as self-deification, so also erotic love and friendship (as the poet understands it, and with his understanding this love stands or falls) are idol-worship. Ultimately, love for God is the decisive factor; from this originates love for the neighbor—but paganism had no inkling of this. It left out God, made erotic love [*Elskov*] and friendship into love [*Kjerlighed*], and abhorred self-love. But the Christian love commandment commands loving God above all else, and then loving the neighbor. In erotic love and friendship, preferential love is the middle term; in love for the neighbor, God is the middle term.[7]

In contrast, imperative love begins with obedience to God's command. Love begins from God's commandments, not from preference. Whereas man's love begins by preference and results in self-satisfaction, imperative love obeys the commandments and gains God. The goal of human love is self-satisfaction, while the ultimate goal of imperative love is God. Therefore, the one who is given imperative love exists only as an object of love and does not exist as the one who satisfies the self-fulfilling needs of the lover. In Christian love, self-gratifying desires are satisfied with eternal life. We are empowered to love our neighbors as our human essential and spiritual needs are fulfilled with eternal life.

Imperative love begins and lasts by will, not by emotions. Since it does not start with emotions, it hardly brings about passion. Generally, a strong will comes out of the passion of love. Christian love, however, builds passion from obedience to the command of

7 Ibid., 57-58.

love. Imperative love does not derive its passion from emotions, but it has a spiritual passion for obtaining eternity. Therefore, the human flesh can attain spiritual and physical harmony by submitting to the passion of the spirit.

What does this mean? In Christian love, the condition for passion, namely "do with all your heart, your will and your mind" is given. Passion comes from thorough obedience. Then how can this contrived and intentional will be love? We obey the command to love our neighbors through the commandment to love God with all our heart, our will, and our mind. However, this passion does not naturally arise in man. Man is only passionate for the self-fulfilling love that satisfies himself. Therefore, we cannot expect any passion when loving our neighbors because our intrinsic passion is directed only toward ourselves. When loving neighbors, we will develop an ability to love in our mortal flesh through obedience only to the commandments of the Spirit, not to our innate passion. By obeying the command to "pour out all your heart, will, and mind," love is safeguarded against ever-changing preferences and becomes an independent, unchanging value of eternal love.

It is only in love for the neighbor that the self, who loves, is defined as spirit purely spiritually and the neighbor is purely spiritual specification. Therefore what was said at the beginning of this discourse does not hold true at all for erotic love and friendship—namely, that only one human being acknowledged as the neighbor is needed in order to cure one of self-love. If in that person one loves the neighbor.[8]

As we begin to love as an attempt to gain the reality of God, we practice and expand our truth that "love is eternal," which does not exist in man by obeying imperative love. We also realize that only this obedience is the reality of self-denial. Why? In order for love to be eternal, it cannot follow man's own standards and self-desires that change according to preferences. Love becomes eternal only when we abandon our desires and choose the truth that "love is eternal."

A person who can love with Christian love is the one who obeys the commandment to love his neighbor. While loving his neighbors, he expands God in himself. Anyone who expands the love of God

8 Ibid., 56-57.

by self-denying obedience gains eternal life, which is knowing God and Jesus Christ whom He has sent. Unlike preferential love that constantly changes the object of preference, Christian love is the life of God that truly fills oneself and overflows to others and saves them.

When the lover or friend is able to love only this one single person in the whole world (which is a delight to the poet's ears), there is an enormous self-willfulness in this enormous devotion, and in his impetuous, unlimited devotion the lover is actually relating himself to himself in self-love. Self-denial wants to root out this self-love, this self-willfulness, by means of eternity's *you shall*.[9]

9 Ibid., 55.

Chapter 4

Love achieves equality

Giving greater honor to the part that lacked it (1 Cor. 12:24)

Preferential love changes because it lacks eternity. But imperative love does not begin with an attempt to satisfy capricious human needs, but it begins as **"going with God (and it is indeed only in this company that one discovers *the neighbor*, because God is the middle term) in order to know life and oneself is an earnest walk."**[10] In other words, Christian love begins with the desire to walk with God to understand the relationship between eternal life

10 Ibid., 77.

and man. Loving one's neighbor in Christianity is the great will of God that is given to a person who is connected to God and the great purpose of human existence in which the person becomes one's true self in eternity.

The main difference between preferential and imperative love is that the former is based on the purity of emotion, whereas the latter begins with the premise that "none of us is pure humanity."[11] Imperative love, therefore, begins with learning love from God who is the essential love. If anyone denies the reality of God, the definition of love will begin with man. But for man, love is not our nature, but just an act that we do. There is still a lack when love starts from man. In imperative love, man is made into love by recognizing the existence of God who is the essence of love.

The lovers no doubt think that in erotic love they have the highest, but this is not so, because in it they still do not have the eternal secured by the eternal ... In contrast, the *royal Law*, the love commandment, promises

11 Ibid., 70.

life, eternal life, and this commandment simply says, "You shall love your neighbor." Just as this commandment will teach everyone how to love oneself, so it also will teach erotic love and friendship genuine love:[12]

Imperative love transcends any discrimination brought by preferences. The goal of imperative love lies not in the benefit from loving the neighbor but in being connected to God by obeying the command. Preferential love is defined by the condition of the loved one. For example, if I love "a girl with a long hair," the condition of love is limited to having a long hair and love stops as soon as the long hair is shortened. However, imperative love is eternal because it is not restricted to the condition of the object of love and obeys the commandment. As long as we choose imperative love, we are connected to God.

How can imperative love be associated with God? Imperative love overcomes the despair that stops love. Preferential love for "the long-haired girl" stops when the hair is shortened unless the condition

12 Ibid., 61-62.

of preference is restored. Imperative love, however, always owns eternity through obedience to the commandment, overcoming despair because there is no condition of preference. In this sense, imperative love is the only way for mortal man to be enduringly connected to the eternal God.

Furthermore, only imperative love can define man as love without discrimination. In imperative love, man is only "the object of love." If there is no God who is the essence of love in this universe, who can define human beings as "the objects of love?" He who obeys imperative love becomes a partaker of the great work of God, who is rich in all things, makes man the subject of His love, and pours out His eternal love. Thus, it is the greatest work that man can do to love the neighbor because only in this place is man connected to the eternal God and only in this glorious place does man, as His instrument, witness God's eternal love in which He pours out His all.

Truly, only by loving the neighbor can a person achieve the highest, because the highest is to be able to be an instrument in the hand of

Governance.[13]

Why is this love so great? The eternal nature of imperative love brings ultimate equality to man by overcoming all discriminatory factors in man. The world is not equal. There are rich and poor people, and there exist ranks and classes. In this diversity, preferential love is very fragile. People who do not have any preferential condition are less likely to be loved. But imperative love fills all human differences with love.

Man chooses love to be connected to the eternal God, and God's riches are poured out on this earth through those who have chosen God. The reason why love should be the willful obedience to the command "you shall love" (the definition of love) is as follows: Man chooses love for the purpose of gaining eternity and God. Since man's love is not essential love, man does not have the natural desire to love without favorable conditions. God, the Creator, who is essential love itself, however, wants to fill the deficiency of this earth

13 Ibid., 86.

with never-failing and abundant love, ultimately revealing the eternal nature of God on earth. In other words, the will to love is the will of God. Man has no power to fill deficiencies.

Without connection to God, man will wear out by trying to make up for the deficiencies. It might be arrogant to make such an effort. The inadequacy of the world can only be overcome by an outpouring of eternal life through a person who obeys the command to love. At this point, we can see why belief in the existence of God is necessary for imperative love. The will to love is the will of the Creator. When we obey the commandment, we will participate in the Creator's will to love. Since love is the will of the Creator, love will not stop as long as man obeys it.

However ludicrous, however frustrating, however inexpedient loving the neighbor may seem in the world, it is still the highest a person is capable of doing.[14]

---

14 Ibid., 86.

Chapter 5

Love is the fulfillment of the law

Man is connected to God by choosing love. Christian love begins when man is connected to God, the truth. The reality of this connection to God is the law (God's commandment). The relationship between man who is not love and God who is the body of love is only possible when man leaps to the essence of love. This desire to leap begins with the belief that love exists, and the realization that human love is motivated by self-love.

The love of Christianity is a leap from man's "existential emptiness" to the Creator's "abundance of everything." According to this premise, man achieves the love of God as much as he makes a leap into love. God has enabled this leap to begin with the commandment, "you shall love." Obedience to this command is only possible when we realize the undeniable truth about human existence. That is, man is not love and is full of emptiness to be filled.

Without such a consensus on human existence, man will not obey the commandment because he will continue to give preferential love by defining the existing standards of self-love as genuine love. The command "you shall love" is an invitation to gain genuine love from the Being who is love. It is also a call for obedience to the command because it is a way that man would never choose considering that man is unable to love anyone but himself. Why is it then a command, not an exhortation and an obedience, not a choice?

An order brings about an action whose outcome is guaranteed by the person who gives the order. If the result of an order is the same as the result of persuasion, there is no reason to give an order. An order can be given by an authority that guarantees absoluteness and certainty, and submission to the order is an action shown by a person who follows it with trust. The command to love is an expression of certainty that man's existential futility will be filled with love, and that "the being of nothingness" will be filled with "life and eternity." Therefore, both standard and completion of love are given by the commander. We begin our journey by a leap to the absolute standard which the Creator cannot lower.

To truly love oneself is to love God. To love God is to love oneself in the truth.

The only way for man to truly love himself is to leap to God. That is, being connected to God by obeying the command of love is to love God, and at the same time, it is an act of loving oneself the most. This love begins with a person who loves himself most by loving God. Those who acquire eternal life by being connected to God will love others who are stuck in "existential futility." This love is essentially different from human love. Man naturally chooses love to satisfy himself. But this love invites man to the way of fulfillment because the inviter is overflowing already. For this reason, this love is the purest love that is not motivated by self-interest.

But the challenge that this love faces is that the world does not know and cannot even imagine the richness of this inner world. Love begins to be misunderstood. When giving love that will lead to a leap, we must first remind our beloved ones that "man who is not love needs God." The problem is that people who are only used to preferential love acknowledge being loved as having a favorable condition.

There are two dilemmas here. One is that the love of the truth is blurred due to compromise with worldly people who are familiar with preferential love and secondly that those who want to obey the command are tempted to receive good reputations. This is the most difficult dilemma for those who want to convey true love. What is important here is that this love is a command. It is a command that must be obeyed continually until the demands of the law are fulfilled. Kierkegaard said that when love is not a command, love always stays in despair. It means that love does not last. If we succumb to this temptation, the first thing that we lose is God because we lost eternity by quitting love.

> The essentially Christian is this: truly to love oneself is to love God; truly to love another person is with every sacrifice (also the sacrifice of becoming hated oneself) to help the other person to love God or in loving God.[15]

Another dilemma is that the more faithful the one who obeys is to the command, the more misunderstood he will be. A person who is led to "love God" will be first awakened to the fact that every person's miserable condition is that "you are not love and do not have any condition to be loved by God." Practically, it is like giving a message that "you have no preferential conditions" and that "you are not a person to be loved at all."

Who will do such love? As I said above, only those who obey the command can act in true love. He is a person who submits to the absolute authority of God with absolute confidence. How can he live such a life? Remember! He started this journey out of his existential despair. His obedience is an act of "truly loving himself." He is connected to God through obedience and gains God so that he never

15 Ibid., 114.

wants to weaken "truly loving himself," nor does he want to disobey it.

First, even if the object of love misunderstands his love and does not accept it, he will continue to obey. This is because, as I said above, this obedience is the act of "truly loving oneself." Second, he loves the truth of God. His love for God is strong enough to overcome misunderstanding and hatred because God is truthful. Only love that does not despair acquires eternity, and love that endures completes love. What he wants to accomplish is love of the truth in him before he loves neighbors. Accordingly, he continues to love.

To love God is to love oneself truly; to help another person to love God is to love another person; to be helped by another person to love God is to be loved.[16]

The second reason for his obedience is as follows: to be truly loved

16 Ibid., 107.

is to help the object of love leap into God's love. This concept is also different from that of general love. In general, to be loved is the result of preference. However, to be loved from a Christian perspective is being filled with God as the object of love accepts God.

Christian love begins and ends with God. Love cannot begin except by God, the essence of love. A person who is not connected to God through a leap cannot give the essential love of Christianity. Christian love is finding God and revealing God's thoughts and character (the law). Anyone who has discovered the true and perfect love of God does not hesitate to defend the true God despite misunderstandings and persecutions. Without God, the truth and reality of life cannot be known. We leap to God by submitting to imperative love so that our lives become increasingly clear in the truth. On the other hand, if we do not obey the command, we cannot know God and human existence falls into doubt and confusion.

To whom every human being, not by birth but by creation from nothing, belongs as a bond servant, and in such a way as no bond servant has ever belonged to an earthly master, who at least admits that thoughts and feelings are free; but he belongs to God in every thought, the most hidden; in every feeling, the most secret; in every movement, the most inward ... If God is dismissed, the place will indeed be vacant. As a reward for such presumption, all existence will in that way probably come closer and closer to being transformed into doubt or into a vortex.[17]

17 Ibid., 115.

Chapter 6

Love is a matter of conscience

Having purified your souls by your obedience to the truth for a sincere brotherly love, love one another earnestly from a pure heart

(1 Pet. 1:22)

The most distinctive feature of Christian love is that it is not separated from God and eternity. In fact, it is no exaggeration to say that Christian love is maintained because of God and eternity. This is also why Christian love has a higher value than ethical or moral love. The command "you shall love" becomes equal to the statement, "you will gain God and eternal life." The more we love, the more we will have a change that will bring about eternal life, the resurrection life of Christ. In this respect, the standard for obtaining the greatest life that can be given to man (eternal life – Jn. 17:3) has to be high.

In order to gain God, we must be in a position to have a relationship with Him and to know Him more. Where does this relationship begin? It begins at "conscience." Man begins a relationship with God through the conscience that exists inside him though it is invisible and cannot be proven. We cannot generalize the inner world of each of us. However, it is clear that our inner world is shaped through our consciences. Now we see the stark difference between preferential and Christian love. Preferential love is for the outer world, and Christian love for the inner world. As for preferential love, there are only the object and subject of love, but Christian love requires God as well as both a subject and an object of love because a person who has started the relationship with God through his conscience approaches another person without discrimination.

How then can Christians love others regardless of preferences? Christians can because this deeply mysterious, secret, and the greatest thing begins inside. First of all, loving God takes place in the mind where conscience is restored. As Christians begin to love God, they are confronted with a dilemma in this secret inner castle,

“Shall I love God?” or “Shall I love myself?” (Preferential love loves oneself exclusively. As preferential love grows, narcissism becomes maximized. Preferential love cannot be considered as genuine love for others, because it cannot overcome favoritism.)

When self-loving man begins a relationship with God by listening to his conscience, it is because he wants what he cannot get by himself but only through God. Eternal life is what we will have when we obey the command. A person who has a relationship with God by listening to his conscience is one who has put down self-love to obey the command of God to gain eternal life. If you are obedient to the truth of the good and righteous God, your relationship with God begins in the inner castle.

Here man continually receives the message of God, “you shall love,” which he obeys. As I mentioned before, imperative love does not co-exist with self-love, but imperative love completes the law. In this journey, your self-love can die and it is the only way to love without deception. In Christian love, “no deception” does not mean the violation of moral law. The agreement we agreed upon when we first began this journey was that this journey is choosing “God” when faced with a conflict between "loving God" and "loving me." Thus, the Christian meaning of "no deception" in love is to be faithful in loving God and not to fall into self-love.

Then, what does "love unfeigned" look like? To love God without deceit is to possess a focused and sincere mind. Kierkegaard said that the mind that focuses on God is bound to God, and the opposite is the free mind that indulges in favor of the self. The mind that is bound to God is not a mind that follows the desire of the self. Literally, the mind is bound to the will of God. However, the more we are bound to God, the more we are free from our own desires (not enslaved to ourselves and free in the truth). In this inner castle, there is only one master. When in the face of choice there is always a fight between the desire of the self and the commandments of God, it is evidence of a confused and false mind. As the mind is firmly, continually, and unbrokenly bound to God, the human mind becomes pure. A free mind, however, cannot obtain anything because it is not bound to anything.

A pure heart is not a free heart in this sense, or it is not what is under consideration here, since a pure heart is first and last a *bound heart* ... A bound heart, yes, in the deepest sense a bound heart — namely, that heart must be bound to God ... but the heart, if it is to be pure, must without limit be bound to God ... God does not die, and the bond that binds is never broken.[18]

This cleansed heart that is bound to God bears the fruit of "faithfulness to obedience." The purer heart you have, the clearer the will of God will be. This is because the energy that leads man to self-desire is weakened and finally vanishes. As a result, we love God more, which results in unconditional love for mankind. To reach this conclusion, there are two conditions that we should not overlook. The first is the element of self-deception and the second is the possibility of insincerity. Kierkegaard is adamantly saying that a person without self-knowledge cannot love without deception. In summary, it is difficult for a person without self-knowledge to know the danger of self-deception.

18 Ibid., 148.

Is it insincerity only when a person consciously deceives others or himself? Is it not also insincerity when a person does not know himself? Indeed, can such a person promise love out of a sincere faith, or can he—keep what he promises? Yes, that he can, but if he cannot promise, can he then keep what he cannot even promise? The one who does not know himself cannot promise love out of a sincere faith.[19]

When faithfulness in loving God fades away, it is evidence that there is an element of self-love hidden underneath. This can be illustrated with two opposing forces: the power to go out (centrifugal force, loving God) and the power to pull it in (centripetal force, self-love). These two forces cannot move in the same direction. If those two forces exist at the same time, then the direction is lost. When there is no direction, the force stops. Therefore, the centripetal force of insincerity means that self-love has begun, and the presence of that power means the centrifugal force of loving God has come to a stop. Man easily falls into self-deceit that these two forces can co-

19 Ibid., 151.

exist. The coexistence of both powers is the result of self-deception combined with the centripetal force of self-love.

A sincere faith. Would any more revolting combination be possible than loving—and falsity? But it is, of course, an impossibility, because to love falsely is to hate. This holds true not only for falsity but it is impossible to join the slightest lack of honesty with loving. As soon as there is any lack of honesty, there is also something concealed, but selfish self-love hides itself in this concealment, and insofar as this is present in a person, he does not love.[20]

When we go beyond self-deceit to belong to the centrifugal force of loving God, we will continue to choose the truth (loving God) through the heart redeemed by God, and we will produce the fruit of loving our neighbors earnestly. Now we have come to the place of obeying God by accepting the definition that "loving is choosing God." Our obedience does not restrain our liberty because the

20 Ibid., 151.

bondage is a heart that is surrendered to God because of love, and the result is the blessing of eternal life, which can never be attained by man's narcissistic efforts.

Behold, how good and pleasant it is when brothers dwell in unity! It is like the precious oil on the head, running down on the beard, on the beard of Aaron, running down on the collar of his robes! It is like the dew of Hermon, which falls on the mountains of Zion! For there the Lord has commanded the blessing, life forevermore.[21]

21 Ps. 133:1-3

Chapter 7

Love is duty

That they may all be one, just as you, Father, are in me, and I in you, that they also may be in us, so that the world may believe that you have sent me. The glory that you have given me I have given to them, that they may be one even as we are one, I in them and you in me, that they may become perfectly one, so that the world may know that you sent me and loved them even as you loved me. (Jn. 17:21-23)

The love of Christianity became visible when God sent His only begotten Son. The evidence that God so loved the world is His Son Jesus. Jesus was the only being who saw God and can be a witness to who God is. What Jesus wanted us to know was the relationship with God, and to have the same relationship of togetherness with God by receiving Jesus. Why does love have to be an obligation in Christian salvation? To understand this, we need to look at the meaning of Jesus' love for man.

The fact that Jesus is God means that He is a perfect being. And the fact that Jesus as the Savior loved a sinner means that man is imperfect. Thus, it is a logical conclusion that Jesus' love for man cannot be the love of preference. When we understand love as preference, we look for people with conditions that we can love. However, the love that Jesus showed indicates that no condition of preference can be found in man. A perfect being cannot favor an imperfect being. In this sense, Christian love depends entirely on the nature of God, "God is love." It means that the basis of love is the character and power of God's love. What is the purpose of salvation? It is ultimately the restoration of the image of God destroyed by sin. Accordingly, the purpose of God's love for man is the restoration of human beings who can love others like God. The love we receive is marvelous love that completes man, in which the perfect love of God pours out into imperfect man.

This means that Christian love begins with God. A man who is restored by love because God loves him is given the duty of imperative love from God. Here we find the legitimacy of the duty of imperative love. In Christian love, the obligation of imperative love shapes a person's character through the process of carrying out the obligation. Man has to take God's demand for love as an obligation because man is only accustomed to receiving love. There is no reason for an imperfect man not to desire unity with the perfect Jesus Christ. However, this imperative love must begin as an obligation that has to be accomplished with one's will in order for an intrinsically incomplete human being to love another man who is not love essentially as God is. Christ's love for man is completed to the end because He is love, but man's love for a neighbor builds character when love begins as an obligation and is accomplished by will.

To embody the reality of perfect love in a human soul, we must accept loving our neighbor as an obligation. Kierkegaard says, "In the human sense, to be absolutely certain of being loved is not to love."[22] Absolute assurance of God's love is impossible because it is earned in proportion to the extent of how much we love. Therefore, a person who is absolutely convinced that he is being loved by God shows the self-deception of man who has never tried mandatory

---

22 Ibid., 156.

love. By doing obligatory love, we are realistically convinced of God's love. Confidence in the love of God gets stronger in accordance with how much we achieve obligatory love in our lives.

We must now start practicing mandatory love for the completion of our salvation. The biggest temptation when doing mandatory love is to seek the efficiency of love. We tend to find objects so that our love can be done meaningfully and appropriately. However, we have to resist this temptation for two reasons. First, this temptation is a kind of narcissism like preferential love. Second, the authenticity of love is proven by how much our love is wasted. The purpose of compulsory love is to love others in the same manner as we have received. In this regard, this love has to be an outpouring from the one who has Christian love to the one with deficiency. The inefficiency is a natural outcome in this structure. If we try to be perfect and effective, we will never find the object of love.

Christian love, however, comes down from heaven to earth. Thus the direction is the opposite. Christian love is not supposed to soar up to heaven, since it comes from heaven and with heaven. It comes down and thereby accomplishes loving the same person in all his changes, because it sees the same person in all the changes.[23]

Therefore, a person who can love in a Christian way is someone who is loved by Jesus Christ and knows and loves Him. Whether man loves God is determined by obedience to the command. Those who are willing to practice this imperative love are those who love God. At this point, we must not forget that Jesus is in us as God is in Jesus ("I in them and you in me, that they may become perfectly one" (Jn. 17:23)). The fact that Jesus is in us is revealed when we obey imperative love. We must remember that Jesus' perfect love is dwelling in us. If we forget the resource of perfect love, which we have in ourselves and seek to find the source of love from ourselves, we are again driven to preferential love. The result is a lack of love.

Everyone is the object of love for those who remember the love of the cross and try to complete the amazing love in themselves. For them, there is only love to convey. The love is pure and powerful only

---

23 Ibid., 173.

when there is no condition for love. When we obey the demands of this obligatory love and realize the meaning of this love, the love of Jesus abides in us as real power. The Word that we are one with Jesus as He is in us becomes the reality.

Because the inability to find any object for one's love among people amounts to denouncing oneself as totally lacking in love. Is this indeed love, to want to find it outside oneself? I thought that this is love, to bring love along with oneself. But the one who brings love along with himself as he searches for an object for his love (otherwise it is a lie that he is searching for an object—for his love) will easily, and the more easily the greater the love in him, find the object and find it to be such that it is lovable. To be able to love a person despite his weakness and defects and imperfections is still not perfect love, but rather this, to be able to find him lovable despite and with his weaknesses and defects and imperfections.[24]

24 Ibid., 158-159.

Only when we obey the command that love is an obligation should we seek to find conditions to love in everyone. When love is a command to be accomplished, we can love all humans whose preferential love fails to love because of a lack of love. The condition for love here is the condition to receive love, not the condition of preference. In other words, only those who have enough love to fill themselves can put all people in the place of love. The condition is also a condition to be loved because there is fullness of love that can overflow to all people. There is no greater power of love than this.

> Would it not be even sadder, as well as even more confused, if love, too, would be only a course because its requirement could only make it obvious that none of us is worth loving, rather than that love would be known by the very fact that it is loving enough to be able to find something lovable in all of us, that is, loving enough to be able to love all of us![25]

25 Ibid., 158.

Chapter 8

We are indebted to love

Now his older son was in the field, and as he came and drew near to the house, he heard music and dancing. And he called one of the servants and asked what these things meant. And he said to him, 'Your brother has come, and your father has killed the fattened calf, because he has received him back safe and sound.' But he was angry and refused to go in. His father came out and entreated him, but he answered his father, 'Look, these many years I have served you, and I never disobeyed your command, yet you never gave me a young goat that I might celebrate with my friends. But when this son of yours came, who has devoured your property with prostitutes, you killed the fattened calf for him!' And he said to him, 'Son, you are always with me, and all that is mine is yours. It was fitting to celebrate and be glad, for this your brother was dead, and is alive; he was lost, and is found.' (Lk. 15:25-32)

Christian love begins with God, the essence of love, and is completed by the obedience of Jesus Christ. We receive God's infinite love and at the same time actualize it through the obedience of self-denial. We come to know that love is an infinite debt which ought to be repaid by giving all only through the love of God. Through the example of the prodigal son in the Book of Luke, we can think about the debt of love from various angles.

We are deeply touched by the amazing love of the Father from the point of view of the prodigal son who has no conditions to receive his father's love, but we often stay in his big brother's position, comparing his works with the prodigal brother, without knowing that he is the one who owes the infinite love. How can we become an infinite debtor of love in this situation? From the worldly point of view, being loved is owing a debt, but from a Christian point of view, the subject of love owes the debt of love. This is because only the person who loves rather than the one who receives love finds out the reality of love. Christian love comes to us as the great task to present the purpose and direction of life. Its task is to fill all the deficiencies of a neighbor with love so that eternal life continues to exist in us.

It is important to remember that this task of love assigned to us is essentially for our own sake. Only by love can we be connected to God. If one truly wants to actualize God's love in this world, he will love others and come to understand the debt of love received from God. He will never want to stop loving others because the more he loves, the more he will appreciate this love. If this treasure hunt of finding the love of God by loving others is the task of love, who would want to give up the treasure? If we do not pay the debt of love by practicing the task of love in our lives, we will never know the reality of God and His love we believe in.

We have to remember in Christian love that we are not love yet. We can constantly maintain the vitality of love only through obeying the command and fulfilling the obligation of love. To maintain the vitality of love, we need to remember the nature of love once more. Christian love cannot be separated from "God and eternity." In order to maintain the vitality of love not disconnected from God and eternity, we must remember that the object of love is God and that our choices should have the eternal nature. Conversely, when humans, who are not love, change the object of love from God to self, and limit the capacity of love to human standards, away from the limitless choice of completing love, love will lose its vitality.

Everything that is to be kept alive must be kept in its element; but love's element is infinitude, inexhaustibility, immeasurability. Therefore, if you want to maintain your love, you must see to it that love, caught for freedom and life, continually remains in its element by means of the infinitude of the debt; otherwise it wastes away and dies—not sooner or later, because it dies immediately, which is precisely a sign of its perfection, that it can live *only* in infinitude.[26]

When we begin to embody the object of love into ourselves, love ceases. The big brother of the prodigal son is a good example here. He forgot that he is his father's infinitely loved child and began to count his work as evidence of loving his father. If he had come to love and obey his father by realizing his father's unconditional love, everything he did would have become a driving force to love his father deeply. By doing so, he would have realized the amazing love of his father and whatever belonged to his father was his. However, he forgot that the command of love is a task and fell into self-centered love where he wanted to count his work and receive his father's love according to how much work he did. What he still does not know is the reality of his father's love and its abundance.

If he had been earnestly obedient to the task of love, and if he had been in the place of the great love in which he owes love by loving, he would have seen the love he had received when his father

---

26 Ibid., 180.

accepted the prodigal son and realized that the banquet prepared for the prodigal son had already been prepared for him. But he lost the vitality of love because he was concentrating on self-centered love by counting, and he had no more than the heart of a worker, not the firstborn son of a wealthy father. The premise of Christian love begins with the fact that we are already loved. We cannot even know the love we have received by downgrading it to something that we can pay back self-centeredly.

> And thus only to exist or to continue to exist, ... Thus when love dwells on itself, it must be in its particular expression that it becomes itself an object, or that another separate love becomes the object ... When the object is a finite object in this way, love dwells on itself, inasmuch as *infinitely* to dwell on itself is indeed to move. But when love dwells finitely on itself, all is lost.[27]

It is human nature to count our love for others. However,

---

27 Ibid., 182.

calculations attempted by humans are often wrong. First of all, Christian love pays others back for the love, which we owe to God. In this sense, our love is a repayment of our debt to God, love that cannot be counted to the object of love. If someone makes such an attempt, it cannot be love. The reason is as follows: preferential love is the result of self-satisfaction, and imperative love is the result of the existence of God's love realized through the vitality of love. Thus, to get self-satisfaction from imperative love is to reveal that this love does not belong to either of the two loves. It is like a businessman who wants to sell goods without any losses.

Christian love is not such cheap love. The love of Christianity is great in the following aspects. First, God is the one who will count the imperative love we give to others as we obey Him. The object of love has to be God for us to obey the command. Second, imperative love protects us from self-centered calculations and enables us to maintain the vitality of love continually. It is God Himself that counts our obedience to the love we have given. Thus, imperative love prevents corruption and makes Christian love pure.

Whoever is generous to the poor lends to the Lord, and he will repay him for his deed.[28]

Why does God want to bring humanity to love in this way? It is like the heart of the prodigal son's father, which is to let the older son know that everything the father has belongs to the son who lives with him. God wants us (who are not love) to have eternal life by choosing love and makes it possible for us to complete the love of God. The love of God is stronger than death. Because of this love, man was saved without any condition, even though man died in all his transgressions and sins. What we do not know yet, however, is the reality of this incredible and amazing love of God.

Only when we obey the command of infinite, incomprehensible and immeasurable love of God, can we understand the love of God who has already given it to us. God does want you to know His great and noble heart who loves man to the end with the will of love stronger than death in spite of all the deficiencies, insufficiencies and

---

28 Prov. 19:17

stubbornness of human beings. God, the essence of love, is rich in all good things. His unending love does not become weary, and is never insufficient. There is no creature that cannot be filled with Him. God makes us know the reality of the debt that we cannot pay for and makes us dwell in the fullness of God by commanding unlimited love to neighbors.

Its [Christianity's] intention is not to work love weary far from it, but Christianity, by virtue of its eternal nature and with the earnestness of eternity, knows that it is able to manage love, and for this reason it speaks very simply and is very earnest about the matter—just as the iron-willed riding master who knows that he can manage the horse does not admire its fieriness but says that it is supposed to be fiery. He does not take the fieriness away from the horse but by controlling the fieriness only refines it. In the same way Christianity knows how to control love and to teach it that there is a task at every moment.[29]

29 Ibid., 189.

Chapter 9

The challenge of love

Whoever speaks, as one who speaks oracles of God; whoever serves, as one who serves by the strength that God supplies—in order that in everything God may be glorified through Jesus Christ. To him belong glory and dominion forever and ever. Amen. (1 Pet. 4:11)

Love is strong as death (Song 8:6)

Christian love begins with those who possess the eternal life of God as they obey imperative love. We have chosen love to have eternal life, and by choosing love we now own God and eternity. This life is the life of God and is delivered through Jesus Christ (Jn. 17:3). This life enables man to love God, not himself. Fleshly life loves man himself while God's spiritual life loves God. Through obedience to imperative love, only those who follow God's spiritual desire can love God.

The love we pursue leads us to gain God's life by obeying the command, and to seek the will of God. What is the will of God? It is to love God and love man. We began to love God by obeying the commandments[30] and now we are in a position to love man. Then, how does Christian love begin? It begins with faith in the presence of love that does not regard any preconditions. We come to believe in the existence of love as we have faith in the existence of God. Love exists because God is love. The love of truth we pursue is possible because we believe in the presence of love.

> What then, is love? Love is to presuppose love; to have love is to presuppose love in others; to be loving is to presuppose that others are loving.[31]

The premise that love exists is important because we are in a place to love others and we are about to start loving a person in whom we cannot find any preference that "this man is so lovable." We are trying to give imperative love, not self-gratifying love. Why does

30 1 Jn. 5:3

31 Ibid., 223.

God want us to love? The reason is that the truth of God is realized through the love that we accomplish. The reality of the love we believe in is manifested only through the love we give. If we do not believe in love, we will not start to love, and the reality of the truth we believe will be unknown.

"It is not arrogant, it is not impetuous, it is not irritable." It is not arrogant in the opinion that it should create love in the other person, ...[32]

We begin to love our neighbors with the will to embody the truth. Christian love, whose purpose is to embody love in the object of love, begins with the belief that the image of God exists in man. Of course, you cannot see the visible image yet. As we believe that man was created by the image of God, we can begin our love believing that the invisible image of God is engraved in the human soul. Christian love is based on the belief in the creation and in the mind of God imprinted in His creatures. This love consists of the strong will to

32 Ibid., 221-222.

love, which is stronger than death, and is accomplished by those who aspire to reveal the reality of truth by embodying love.

> *"Love believes all things,"* because to believe all things means to presuppose that love, even though it is not seen—indeed, even though the opposite is seen—is still present in the ground, even in the misguided, even in the corrupted, even in the most hateful. Mistrust takes away the very foundation by presupposing that love is not present—therefore mistrust cannot build up.[33]

A person whose goal is to reveal the reality of the truth of God sees his neighbor as the object to which this love has to be poured out. Therefore, the lack of favorable conditions of loved ones does not matter. The lack of a favorable condition is rather an opportunity to fully reveal the richness of God's love. The person giving love does not seek any condition to love except for the eternal life that is in himself. His resources are the presence of God who dwells in his

33 Ibid., 221.

soul. It is the love of Christianity that believes that the never-drying fountain in a Christian's soul can fill any deficiency resulting from destruction.

The subject of love does not despair when he sees the destruction of the object of his love. If a person who wants to practice Christian love falls into despair in the face of human destruction, it proves that he is actually loving with mere preferential love. Christian love begins with the existence of God and is completed by the will of the subject of love. This love is realized by the obedience of those who believe in God's love. He tries to actualize love by giving love to the loved one without being influenced by the loved one's condition. But the process is not easy. Essentially, this process is like a journey that offers an opportunity of tasting the existence of love to those who have never experienced such love before because of destruction. If love is a visible thing, it will be easier to visualize. Love being a matter of faith makes the whole task much harder. If the object of love does not believe all the love he received on the basis of his inner destruction even though the person practicing Christian love has never stopped loving, love does not exist at least for the one who does not believe in such love.

The more perfect the loving one presupposes the love to be, the more perfect a love he loves forth ... it (love) is eternally confident of the fulfillment of the presupposition; if this is not the case, then love is on the way to being exhausted.[34]

Despite tricky risks and difficulties, Christian love has to be carried out because the truth is actualized in the person who practices Christian love. Ultimately, it is inside of those who perform love where love is materialized. In this sense, this love is a journey which entirely depends on the person seeking love of the truth. He will accomplish this journey with patience. At the base of the patience is the belief in the existence of love. He can face the betrayal, misunderstanding, and anger of others, even though he has loved them altruistically and endlessly. However, the reaction of the loved one, which often discourages the subject of love, cannot depress the

34 Ibid., 219.

will of the subject. All these disheartening factors are a challenge to believe that love is still alive and present, and the subject of love continues to answer that question and makes a commitment to Christian love to realize this love in his life.

> Can one human being implant love in another human being's heart? No, this is a suprahuman relationship, an inconceivable relationship between human beings; in this sense human love cannot build up. It is God, the Creator, who must implant love in each human being, he who himself is Love.[35]

Even if all attempts of love made by the person seem to have failed, he is not a failure. Despite the seemingly unsuccessful results, the person himself, who has accomplished love with patience and perseverance, is the reality of truth. Furthermore, it is the existence of God that has led him to this place. Christianity is not afraid of the failure while performing Christian love. The conclusion of love is

35 Ibid., 216.

the life of a man who has attempted giving love. His life is proof that there is a Creator, and that He has planted that love in man. If God does not exist, how can humans attempt to believe that love exists?

> Love is the ground of everything. No human being can place the ground of love in another person's heart; yet love is the ground, and we can build up only from the ground up; therefore we can build up only by presupposing love. Take love away—then there is no one who builds up and no one who is built up.[36]

36 Ibid., 224.

Chapter 10

Love believes everything

Anyone who does not love does not know God, because God is love.

(1 Jn. 4:8)

1. Innerness is important for Christian love

Love that believes everything as in Christian love is different from believing everything in a general sense, which is the result of innocence and ignorance. In order to understand the difference between the two, it is important to know that the challenge for Christian love is the result of a relationship with God, which begins in the innermost being of man. The encounter with the absolute goodness of God gives man the criteria of absolute truth. Only this is the right standard to know God and to have a relationship with Him. One of the evidences that human beings were created in the image of God is that when a person meets God, he begins to have a desire for righteousness to resemble God, although he has been in self-satisfying love. Until the desire of this new life arises by the indwelling Spirit, intrinsically instinctive humans find it hard to believe in goodness. The reason is that there is no absolute goodness in man. For him, goodness means self-satisfaction.

If we were able with unconditioned truth to judge every human being according to a universally given criterion, then the God-relationship would be essentially abolished, then everything would be oriented exteriorly and find its completion paganly in political or social life, then living would become too easy but also exceedingly empty, then the effort as well as the self-deepening that develop the God-relationship in a human being in the most difficult collision of infinite misunderstanding would be neither possible nor necessary, and yet precisely in the most difficult collision of infinite misunderstanding the God-relationship develops in a person.[37]

37 Ibid., 230.

However, those who have tasted the life of God through regeneration will now seek "the righteousness of God," a desire spawned by eternal life. This desire deepens and expands the human mind. Such effort gives true satisfaction. The greater the will for the righteousness of God, the greater the desire for the good. This desire cultivates the inner being of man, gradually achieving the wholeness of inner self and revealing the reality of truth, "the Word became flesh" (Jn. 1:14). The purpose of Christian love is a challenge and a determination to actualize the truth of God in man's inner side. Therefore, this love is not a natural action resulting from innocence and ignorance about the world's evil.

> In relation to everything that is not love, therefore in relation to every deception, true love is unconditionally the superior; consequently it can never be deceived if through believing all things it remains true to itself or continues to be true love.[38]

---

38 Ibid., 236.

A person who practices Christian love tries to trust everything, even though he knows the destruction of the world and all possibilities of evil and darkness. His knowledge of evil comes from himself. That is why he can try to love, willingly believing everything, as opposed to believing what he can believe. In the world, there is relative good and evil, such as what is trustworthy, what is unreliable, what is evil, and what is deceitful. Accordingly, the love that believes everything which Christianity pursues is different from the conclusion arrived at when we examine the relationship between the relative good and the relative bad in this world. We generally believe that evil wins in the world. It is explained by the fact that doubtful people outnumber believing people. It is true. Often attempts to love are defeated by the deception of the wicked. That is why we refuse to undergo such frustration and are generally negative about the love that believes everything.

The truly loving one, who believes all things, cannot be deceived, *because to deceive him is to deceive oneself.* What, namely, is the highest good and the greatest blessedness? Certainly it is truly to love, and next, truly to be loved. But then it is indeed impossible to deceive the one who loves, who by believing all things remains in love.[39]

Christian love is indeed different. When we define Christian love as "love that does not seek its own benefit," the person who attempts Christian love knows that he will face all manner of human selfishness. He knows that all human beings without God will go to the left, which is "self-interest," and that he who practices the love of Christianity will go to the right, which is exactly the opposite of what all human beings walk.

Why does he make such a choice? He chooses the opposite direction against human selfishness because the way to meet God is opposite to the way most people walk. The fact that he chooses the way of truth, not the way of man, is only the result of the constant challenge to believe in God's goodness. Therefore, choosing goodness and love is an act of faith. When looking at love from this perspective, any man or circumstances that he encounters are

39 Ibid., 239.

merely an opportunity whether to confirm or doubt the truth. For him, human selfishness is not an essential reason either to sustain love or to stop loving. (He continues to expand the reality of God by practicing love that believes everything, so that he is gradually made into eternal love.)

2. The difference between love that believes everything and doubt that believes nothing

We now want to see the difference between the love that believes everything and doubt that believes nothing. As we have seen, the will of Christian love is an act of faith that believes in the absolute good and conforms to His standards. Therefore, goodness and truth are expanded inside of him. For him, knowledge is not the criteria of judgment. He starts a relationship by giving his faith to another person instead of seeking a basis upon which this person is trustworthy. He loves this person on the basis of his standard instead of asking for the same standard from his counterpart because he knows that his standard required in his relationship with God is higher than any standard in the world. Thus, knowledge about who the object of love is will not make any difference for him in giving love. Moreover, he is humble enough to put his judgment on hold, so he does not absolutely trust knowledge. His goal is an embodiment of the truth of God, so his love of believing everything arises from the noble good will for the value he pursues.

> The difficulty is to accomplish the task, to acquire the true conception of love or, more correctly, to become the truly loving one, since he defends himself against illusion precisely by believing all things, fights to keep himself in the true love.[40]

His will for the absolute good makes it possible to love even the one who does not believe anything. If you love someone who does not believe anything with love that believes everything, you can expect two results. First, the loved one comes out of the darkness of doubt by finally believing in the power of love of believing

40 Ibid., 236-237.

everything. Second, the loved one betrays the love by doubting everything through the end. We generally regard the second case as failure. But this is wrong. Christian love never fails. The reason is as follows. If Christian love fails, it is only when we lose faith in God. If you lose faith in God, you will not give Christian love, so this is the result of defeat.

To believe nothing at all is the very border where believing evil begins; in other words, the good is the object of belief, and therefore someone who believes nothing at all begins to believe evil. To believe nothing at all is the beginning of *being* evil, because it shows that one has no good in oneself, since belief is the good in a person that does not come with much knowledge, nor is it necessarily lacking because the knowledge is meager. Mistrust cannot maintain knowledge in equilibrium; it defiles its knowledge and therefore verges on envy, malice, and corruption, which believe all evil.[41]

41 Ibid., 234.

However, the person who gives love that believes everything considers every situation which the doubter suspects as a challenge to his faith, and thus "tries to validate his faith that believes everything." Against circumstances in which man is bound to doubt everything, the only reason he can still believe everything is his belief in the providence of God in which "all things work together for good." That is the belief of the one who puts his judgment down and entrusts God with all judgment.

The one who truly loves, who believes all things, cannot be deceived. In other words, in one sense the one who loves is well aware if someone deceives him, but by refusing to believe it, or by believing all things, he keeps himself in love and in this way is not deceived.[42]

If so, has the doubter who does not believe anything ever been deceived by anyone? A person who believes nothing only believes himself. He uses his judgment as a basis for believing nothing. The

42 Ibid., 239.

knowledge about others, which is the ground for his unbelief, is an outcome rather than a cause for his disbelief. His skepticism is not based on knowledge. He cannot objectively accept any knowledge because he refuses to believe. The fact that the distrustful person will not believe anything based on his own judgment reveals that he is a person who is thoroughly separated from love and basically who believes in evil.

> Knowledge is not mistrust, ... Nor is knowledge love, ... The mistrustful person and the loving person have knowledge in common, and neither is the mistrustful person mistrustful through this knowledge nor is the loving person one who loves through this knowledge. But when knowledge in a person has placed the opposite possibilities in equilibrium and he is obliged or wills to judge, then who he is, whether he is mistrustful or loving, becomes apparent in what he believes about it.[43]

43 Ibid., 231.

We need to think about objectivity for a moment. Are objective knowledge and objective judgment possible? A person who chooses Christian love is the one who modifies his subjective frame constantly. He knows that accepting God's truth is the most objective. Most humans, however, consider their subjective thoughts as the truth, so they are basically subjective. How does this subjectivity take shape? In brief, this subjectivity is a framework for humans to see the world. (The only way human beings can escape from this framework is when they leap to the truth.) Then, how does this framework affect us? People see the world with their own frames and receive it back from the world through the same frame. In this respect, it is not possible for us to give love and receive doubt, and give doubt and receive love. As long as man does not suspect whether his will that refuses to believe anything is objective and relies on his knowledge to disbelieve, he will be totally isolated from the good.

Love believes all things.—Light-mindedness, inexperience, naiveté believe everything that is said; vanity, conceit, complacency believe everything flattering that is said; envy malice, corruption believe everything evil that is said; mistrust [*Mistroiskhed*] believes [*tro*] nothing at all; experience will teach that it is most sagacious not to believe everything—but love believes all things.[44]

By disbelieving anything, he does not believe in God and by disbelieving God, he does not believe in goodness, love, and truth. By doing so, he distrusts the possibility of restoring the image of God in himself, and the providence of God in which all things work together for good. By believing in himself only, he loses God, goodness, love, and eternal life. The greatest deception that the person who distrusts anything and doubts everything faces is that he will never know he is the most untrustworthy.

It is mistrust that defiles a person's knowledge, just as love purifies it.[45]

44 Ibid., 226.

45 Ibid., 233.

Chapter 11

Love hopes for everything

So now faith, hope, and love abide, these three; but the greatest of these is love. (1 Cor. 13:13)

Yet Christianity knows only one way [*Vej*] and one resource [*Udvej*], but it does always know the way and the resource. It is with the help of the eternal that Christianity at every moment creates fresh air and a prospect.[46]

The life of man begins with self-satisfaction and ends with self-satisfaction. There is neither love nor eternity here. We are presented with a new path to eternity through Jesus Christ. It is the way to gain

46 Ibid., 246.

eternal life by embodying the truth with love. The fact that there is eternal life clearly teaches us what we should pursue on this earth. It is the way of true love that overcomes all human despair with hope. Love reaches eternity with the help of hope.

> Christianity provides a prospect by speaking metaphorically of this earthly life as the time of sowing and of eternity as the time of harvest.[47]

As long as eternity exists, nothing that is sown on this earth yields the fruit of despair. Despair is the final conclusion that man comes to out of his momentary and finite thought. Christian love, however, does not originate from human thoughts, and it shifts us to the commandment of God's love. Love is like a decision to believe in the existence of God, and hope is to lay the path to eternity based on that faith. Only the subject of love can hope, and the result of that hope can be found in eternity. The fact that the life here is the time of sowing seeds, and the fact that we harvest the results in eternity tells

---

47 Ibid., 247.

us that what we should do is to hope in love eternally. It is God who reaps the results in eternal time.

Christianity offers us a new way, the path of Jesus. This road presents us with the way of self-denial when the world goes after self-satisfaction and self-expansion. Christian self-denial is a way of living for God but dying for oneself. Christian self-denial is love that obeys the command, love that is faithful to obligations, love that completes the law, love that believes everything through the power of love, love that endures everything, and love that hopes for everything. Through each of these processes, we become true love. It is important to remember that the strength that connects us to eternity in each process is hope.

And the world is passing away along with its desires, but whoever does the will of God abides forever.[48]

And those who are wise shall shine like the brightness of the sky above[49]

---

48 1 Jn. 2:17

49 Dan. 12:3

A man who overcomes the temptations of this world, fights the desire of the flesh, and obeys the will of God is the one who submits to the command of Christianity, "you shall love." A man who leads fellow men to the way of Jesus which is the only way to obtain eternal life becomes an eternal star (Dan. 12:3). In order for us to have such a life, we must overcome all despair on this earth with the power of love.

Christianity's hope is eternity, and therefore there are light and shadow, beauty and truth, and above all the distance of transparency in its diagram of existence. Christianity's hope is eternity, and Christ is the Way; his debasement is the Way, but he was also the Way when he ascended into heaven.[50]

If we do not believe in eternity, we have no reason not to go after the self-fulfilling life presented by this world. Christian love, however, makes us pursue inner values such as truth, beauty, true

50 Ibid., 248.

love, true relationship, an integrated self, unity with God, and freedom in truth, not the yoke of a servant. Those who pursue those eternal values are not bound by their external life. Their external life is a tool for inscribing such precious values into a human soul.

The life of Christ is the most justifiable evidence and example. Jesus was rejected for speaking the truth and was blamed for His true love. Although He was the Son of God, He was put to death because of the very same accusation and was misunderstood for breaking the Sabbath day even though he was the Lord of the Sabbath. His humiliation indicates that the truth is neglected in this world and His rejection illustrates that people do not know God.

In order to follow Him, we must come to Him, believing that Jesus who was a carpenter is God, and that he is a human, yet has the power to forgive sins. The life of Jesus is a testimony to how far truth and love are from the values of this world. The way of Jesus is the narrow gate, and those who find it are few (Matt. 7:13-14). However, the way of Jesus condemns this world as falsehood and presents the true path to us. Discarding falsehood and choosing the truth are like passing through the narrow gate like Jesus. But here is our hope. The narrow gate is a way of walking with God, the path full of love and hope. God is the essence of hope.

> Surely the eternal extends over the whole of life and there is and should be hope to the end; then there is no period that is the age of hope, but a person's whole life should be the time of hope! And then they think they are speaking with ample experience about hope—by abolishing the eternal.[51]

If we believe that the outcome of our lives is eternally determined at the crossroads of either salvation or condemnation, divided between grazing and chaffing, between sheep and goats, between the children of God and the children of the devil, we will not be able to treat any flippant attitude toward life such as devious tricks or a loveless heart that casually or carelessly does not want to believe anything. If we believe that God who knows the will and thoughts of the heart is our Judge, our lives will not be swayed by the world

51 Ibid., 251.

that is finite and temporary. Only those who have received salvation prepared by God's righteousness and love will solemnly receive His command to love, "you shall love."

Christian love is eternal, so God wants our physical self to be denied and our spirit to be filled with love. In the journey to complete this love, hope is a good friend that empowers us and always reminds us the direction we should go. Only those who obey the command to love will have hope. When love ceases, hope stops too. When should we hope? Every moment of our lives is the moment to love. Each choice becomes eternal with hope, so hope cannot be stopped. When we give up eternity in this world, man despairs and hope disappears.

But now eternity, surely this is the greatest task ever assigned to a human being, and on the other hand it surely is able to vouch for the next moment.[52]

52 Ibid., 252.

Only those who believe eternity hope for tomorrow. Tomorrow lasts only for those who obey love and choose hope. Tomorrow exists only for those who choose hope today. There is no tomorrow for those who choose despair.

Despair hopes nothing at all for others and love hopes all things.[53]

Despair is the emotion that humans feel when they do not believe in omnipotent beings. The ability to defeat despair is omnipotence. Only those who believe in God can overcome despair and can find hope in God.

One who loves—what a joy for the one who loves that he always dares to hope; what a joy for him that eternity vouches to him that there always is hope. The one who loves, the one who truly loves, does not hope *because* eternity authenticates it to him but he hopes *because* he is one who loves, and he thanks eternity that he dares to hope.[54]

---

53 Ibid., 254.

54 Ibid., 259.

Hope is a gift given only to the person who loves. He enjoys eternal life in this world to the extent he does true love. Only love guarantees eternity. Those who do not love cannot obtain eternity.

He hopes for the possibility of the good for the worst reprobate! He learned this from eternity.[55]

For those who love, the basis of hope is God who created the world from nothingness. God created the world with His words from nothing. Just as a person who loves does not find the basis of love from the object of love, God does not find the basis of hope from man. Thus, Christian love can hope even for the most depraved sinner. Only the power of love makes it hopeful. The process can be explained as follows: the subject of love believes that God can save the dead soul by transforming his heart and giving a new heart.

As long as a person giving love places hope in God, it is God who accomplishes it. If you do not have faith in God, you will not love.

---

55 Ibid., 260.

If you do not love, you will never see eternity. As long as you believe eternity, hope exists forever. It is God who accomplishes love. It is our faith in God, through which God works; it is within our faith that love will triumph eventually, and it is our faith in which eternal time is a time for hope.

Chapter 12

Love is not self-seeking

Whoever loves his life loses it, and whoever hates his life in this world will keep it for eternal life. (Jn. 12:25)

In discussing love that does not seek its own benefits, we must first bear in mind that this love is not possible in human love that man pursues. We must acknowledge that human love in which God is excluded is motivated by gratifying human desires. As human love begins with need and concludes with self-satisfaction, we can say that what it ultimately seeks is its own benefit. The love of Christianity, however, is a paradox that acquires true love by not seeking one's own benefit because the motivation of Christian love is gaining God.

In the case of love seeking its own benefit, greed increases accordingly as love grows. The benefits that a loved one receives are inversely proportional to those of the person giving love. The more I satisfy my greed, the less love the loved one will get. Here the ultimate meaning of love is damaged. Love that satisfies unfulfilled greedy desire is completely selfish. However, Christian love is sacrificial and altruistic love in which the object of love gains full benefit because the one giving Christian love does not seek his own interest. The one who gives Christian love ultimately becomes a true beneficiary of love, not a victim, which is to gain God.

> He who created man in his image so that he might be like him, might become perfect as he is perfect, and thus attain the perfection that is God's own, be like the image that is God's own—does he not seek his own? Indeed, he seeks his own, which is love; he seeks it by giving all things. God is good, and there is only one who is good—God, who gives all things.[56]

56 Ibid., 264.

Christian love breaks the wall of "yours" and "mine" which is a dividing barrier for counting love. How does this happen? In the case of worldly love in which the distinction between "yours" and "mine" is clear, "yours" is denied as much as I desire "mine." As the desire to acquire "mine" grows, "yours" is destroyed. Thus, the result of worldly love that pursues "mine" is selfishness and greed, which is the conclusion of self-love. On the other hand, Christian love is freed from selfishness and greed, which are the essential motives of self-love, by denying "mine" on the inside. Meanwhile, on the outside, it loves "yours," thereby purifying the love and expanding the power of perfect love. Only this love has a perfect direction of love.

Love does not seek its own. The truly loving one does not love his own distinctiveness but, in contrast, loves every human being according to his distinctiveness; but "his distinctiveness" is what for him is ***his own****; that is, the loving one does not seek his own; quite the opposite he loves what is the other's own.*[57]

---

57 Ibid., 269.

Only the spirit's love has the courage to will to have nothing at all, the courage to cancel entirely the distinction "yours" and "mine"; therefore it gains God—by losing its soul.[58]

What is the direction of complete love? It is helping others to meet God. In this direction of love, love does not work if there is any motivation to pursue "mine." If you have the motivation of "mine," even though you are in the direction to lead a person to the love of truth, such love will never make him know God. This is because the motivation of "mine" will change the direction of love. The love that leads to truth will merely become a cause and the direction will be re-directed to self-seeking love, which fulfills one's own desires, and the love of truth will be corrupt. In this sense, the Christian love must not seek one's own benefit in order to gain vitality constantly.

In the world of spirit, precisely this, to become one's own master, is the highest—and in love to help someone toward that, to become himself,

58 Ibid., 268-269.

free, independent, his own master, to help him stand alone—that is the greatest beneficence.[59]

To lead others to God means to help restore the image of God in them. This restoration is the restoration of the self as God originally intended and this is possible only through the love of God. It is a hard work that requires long patience and laborious effort. Nevertheless, if there is no recovery in this direction, humans will not be able to escape from an instinctive and beastly life, keep wandering to fill unfulfilled desires, and never meet God. Man can only be restored through love that is pure and true. Just as a child continues to receive the love of his parents and grows into an adult with a healthy self-image, the human soul is restored to the image of God through the continuous love of God.

This work becomes possible only through the obedience of a person who believes in the truth. God has entrusted this work to human hands. It is not the work of man doing it himself, but the

---

59 Ibid., 274.

work that takes place through those who are connected to God by choosing perfect love and have gained eternal life. In other words, human beings are connected to God through obedience to imperative love, and God's love flows again to others through the connected person. Here human beings are God's co-workers and a path of true love.

The one who loves has understood that it truly is the greatest, the only beneficence one human being can do for another, to help him to stand by himself, to become himself, to become his own master; but he has also understood the danger and the suffering in the midst of the work, and above all the terribleness of the responsibility. Therefore, giving thanks to God, he declares: Now this individual is standing by himself—through my help. But there is no self-satisfaction in the last phrase, because the loving one has understood that essentially every human being indeed stands by himself—through God's help—and that the loving one's self-annihilation is really only in order not to hinder the other person's God-relationship, so that all the loving one's help infinitely vanishes in the God-relationship.[60]

We can see God's wisdom here. There is only one Being, who is the essence of love, who can accomplish perfect love by pursuing his own will. Man, who is not love, cannot have perfect love when he is tied to his will. God who wants to restore the image of God urges us to challenge the love in which we do not seek our own benefits in order to gain true love. From the eternal perspective, what man thinks is in his best interest is only a hindrance to eternity. As long as we are tied to our own benefits, we do not see the value of eternity. So God wants us to leap to this true love. It is possible only by putting down our own selfish desires.

However, we feel fear and anxiety when we are not self-seeking. We think that the more we put down our desires the more we will be used by others. That is probably true. All human beings suffering from a lack of love are hungry for love. If a person puts to death his own benefits, another hungry person will take the love and rejoice

---

60 Ibid., 277-278.

as if he were a victor. There is also a paradox here. We abandon our flesh and acquire the Spirit. In other words, we abandon self-love and acquire the perfect God. For example, when we help a person to become his true self, we help him to restore God's image through hard endeavors. This work is demanding, so it cannot be done through the end if there is any desire to benefit from it. Thus, a person who accomplishes this love to the end is the one whose goal arises not from his benefit, but the restoration of the image of God in the loved one.

Then the wondrous thing occurs that is heaven's blessing upon self-denying love—in salvation's mysterious understanding all things become his, his who had no *mine* at all, his who in self-denial made yours all that was his. In other words, God is all things, and by having no *mine* at all self-denial's love won God and won all things. The person who loses his soul will gain it.[61]

61 Ibid., 268.

Ultimately, the one who gains real benefit is the person who loves. It is because those who are ultimately restored through this laborious work are those who love. He will clearly know the meaning of the image of God, remember numerous people of grace who have endeavored to restore him, and ultimately love God more as the source of this love. Meanwhile, the person who has snatched away such noble love like windfall does not know the value of this love given to him as he thinks that he has won this love with his own strength. He may be carried away in the triumph of being a loved one, or he may consider the love that he receives as a godsend. However, he will never know the purity, nobility and sacrifice of this love until he submits to the demand of this love. Those who challenge true love by not seeking their own benefits gain God, the essence of love, but those who only receive this love see it as good fortune. Who has won the truly genuine love in these two cases?

Is it wasting one's life not to seek one's own? No, in truth this life is not wasted. The one who loves is with blessed joy conscious of this and God is his confidant. In a certain sense his life is completely squandered on existence, on the existence of others.[62]

A person who is not self-seeking is a spiritual person. To survive spiritually, the flesh must die because the spiritual life is maintained only by those belong to God. It is the greatest man who has realized that spiritual survival is the true survival of man. For he now understands that obedience is not the pain of bending his will and has found the way of obtaining eternal life through obedience. He who wants to gain eternal life desires to know God more, the only true God, and Jesus Christ whom he has sent (Jn. 17:3). He who has truly obtained all is the one who has found a way to gain eternal life by consuming all he has in order to lead others to the truth.

62 Ibid., 279.

Chapter 13

Love covers all sins

Above all, keep loving one another earnestly, since love covers a multitude of sins. (1 Pet. 4:8)

But the wisdom from above is first pure, then peaceable, gentle, open to reason, full of mercy and good fruits, impartial and sincere. And a harvest of righteousness is sown in peace by those who make peace. (Jas. 3:17-18)

The love of God is affirmed by Jesus' giving His life to man, and we are indebted to that love. The problem is to extend that love outward. The Bible says, "By this we know love, that he laid down his life for us, and we ought to lay down our lives for the brothers" (1 Jn. 3:16). For Christians, love is a debt that must be paid for, not an option. The repayment of this debt, however, does not ruin us but saves us. We are saved not by giving love but by repaying love that we owe. (This is the way to exchange the fleeting moments which we experience here with eternity itself.)

> Just as the temporal vanishes in time, so also it is only in its characteristics, When however, the eternal is in a human being, this eternal redoubles in him in such a way that every moment it is in him, it is in him in a double mode: in an outward direction and in an inward direction back into itself, but in such a way that his is one and the same.[63]

Why? We know that choosing love is to choose God and to choose eternity. By choosing true love, we gradually discard the things in us that do not belong to love. What is not true love prevents us from leaping into eternity. True love is the only way to obtain the most precious eternity that man can obtain in this finite and futile life. Therefore, we must put down everything that belongs to the fleeting moment.

What is the obstacle to love? It is the antennas of darkness within us. The more antennas we have, the better we will be able to navigate and perceive the sins of others. We can think that it is right to condemn the sins of others at that moment. We tend to also

63 Ibid., 280.

show off our worldly wisdom by revealing sins. For in the world identifying the sins of others and exposing them will earn a person a reputation of being smart and intelligent. However, the man of faith has a different point of view. His ability to pinpoint sin is the result of accumulated knowledge about evil in himself. To the extent he discloses sin in himself, it can be said he has the full possibility and recognition for sin.

For such a person, he is unable to do true love. As long as he regards the wisdom of his evil as knowledge, he cannot pursue love. To him, love that believes everything means ignorance, and hopes for everything is nothing but recklessness. For him who is smart, condemnation is the only conclusion.

At the same moment it (love) goes out of itself (the outward direction), it is in itself (the inward direction); and at the same moment it is in itself, it goes out of itself in such a way that this outward going and this returning, this returning and this outward going are simultaneously one and the same.[64]

The problem is that just as love is retained in me as much as I truly love others, so is condemnation. As much as we condemn others, we are condemned by the same measure. Therefore, we must abandon human wisdom and enter a new way of salvation. The beginning of the path is to remember that to truly love others is the only way to have true love in me. To the extent I deliver a person from evil, I am also saved from evil in me. That is, I am redeemed from my debt only by giving love in repayment. From the worldly perspective, some might criticize Christian love as being self-centered because it seems to give love to others to obtain true love.

However, we cannot say this love is selfish. Selfish love can never be saved because it never denies the self. In Christian love, a person is saved by truly loving another person. It happens simultaneously as the result of eternity. The eternity of God's love makes it possible to save others and me at the same time. An example of this is as follows:

64 Ibid., 280.

Only when we forgive the sins of others can we understand the forgiveness of God or that of others for us. If we refuse to forgive and instead condemn others, the forgiveness of God or others does not become a reality.

It is because the evil in us cannot believe the good that is delivered from the outside. Ultimately I must forgive others in order to be forgiven. If we love others in order to satisfy ourselves, we will never be connected to the love of eternity. For the purpose of saving myself, not only others but also I cannot be saved. Only love that truly loves others will save both the subject and object of love at the same time. Truly loving others is the love of self-denial. Only the soul who receives this true love will be saved, and it is retained in the person who loves as true love because it is the love of self-denial.

At the basis of all *understanding* lies first and foremost an *understanding* between the one who is to understand and that which is to be understood. Therefore knowledge of evil (however much it wants to fool itself and others into thinking that is can keep itself pure, that it is a pure knowledge of evil) still has an *understanding* with evil. If this understanding did not exist, if the knowledgeable one found no pleasure in understanding evil, he would abhor understanding it and then would not understand it either.[65]

The first thing we should try in love is to understand. No one is ignorant enough about evil not to perceive the sin of others. Therefore, it is the beginning of love to try to understand sins we perceive. A person who wants to understand is the one who has already chosen to come down from the court. He comes down from the place of accusation and also from the place of judgement. It is also not befitting to be a defender of a sinner. We do not have enough mercy to defend a sinner yet. What we must realize is that the place where we should stand is the defendant's seat.

In the court of other defendants, we should also be in the position of the defendant, not the lawyer, the prosecutor, or the judge. That is, we should try to understand the sinner, placing ourselves in the same shoes as the sinner. A person who does not try to understand is one who is too confident of his ability to keenly label the inner sins of

65 Ibid., 286.

others without knowing that he has the possibility of committing the same sin, and one who boasts of his knowledge. The benefit he gains is worldly reputation, which is an evidence that he is the wicked because doing evil benefits him.

In the same way, then, such a person, as he himself sinks deeper and deeper, discovers the multitude of sins as greater and greater around him. His eyes are sharpened and armed, alas, not in the sense of truth but rather in the sense of untruth; therefore his outlook becomes more and more prejudiced so that, infecting, he sees evil in everything impurity even in the purest—and this outlook is a kind of consolation to him (what a terrible thought!), because it is a matter of urgency for him to discover the multiplicity to be as limitless as possible.[66]

Then, what is the difference between a person who loves and a person who does not? Is the person who loves ignorant? Not at all! The knowledge to recognize evil is not important to the one who

---

66 Ibid., 286.

loves. For him, what is important is his determination to choose love. He tries to understand because he wants to love, and he refuses to see evil because he wants to understand. He wants to love rather than to try to identify evil. By believing and hoping, he builds the belief in the possibility that the wicked will turn away from evil. Thus, knowledge is not important to him.

For the one who does not love, love has already stopped because there is no will to love. What is left is to throw himself into spiritual death by judging others. There is no possibility of any kind of love for him whose love has stopped. For him, the only reality is the list of sins that are defined by worldly wisdom with which he is also defined. Therefore, he who does not love loses the sense of love and becomes a person who only responds to evil. In the end, he only thinks of evil, rejoices at unrighteousness, and becomes the one without truth. The more he does not love, the more he gets away from salvation and loses eternity.

Just as one by faith *believes* the *unseen* **into** what is seen, so he one who loves by forgiveness *believes* **away** what is seen. Both are faith.[67]

When we choose to love, we enter into the possibilities of infinite love. We believe all things with the help of the power of love and cover others' sins by hoping. It does not mean forgiveness in ignorance but forgiveness through understanding. By understanding and covering sin, we eliminate the possibility of evil that could sprout in our souls. When we entrust the judgment of sin to God and forgive the sin of others, our souls are far from all possibilities of evil influences.

Love hides a multitude of sins, because love prevents the sin from coming into existence, smothers it at birth.[68]

The attempt of a debtor to love saves man from the evil influence which is prevalent in the world. Sin always takes root, grows and

67 Ibid., 295.

68 Ibid., 297.

bears fruit. To condemn sin is like putting a name tag on the tree of sin. It never prevents the tree of sin from growing. Only those who love the good can block the influence of sin with the will to love. Sin loses power by forgiveness and is covered with love. The sin of darkness will never be able to exert influence within the light of love. A person who loves is the most blessed person, both to himself and to this world.

Chapter 14

Love endures forever

And the world is passing away along with its desires, but whoever does the will of God abides forever. (1 Jn. 2:17)

God calls us to eternal life. God is eternal and it is God who has put eternity into man's heart (Ecc. 3:11). Therefore, human beings are the only ones to be invited to eternity as they were created in the image of God. Man is led to eternal life by faith in Jesus Christ, and it becomes more and more abundant by his obedience of the flesh. As the Bible says, God's will is to give love. This love, however, neither fulfills the lust of man nor will end in this world. This love begins only by connection to God and continues by obeying the command of love, so that mortal man is renewed into eternal love. How can man abide forever? It is possible when man is united with God by obedience to the commandment of love. (The union with God is only possible when man gains eternity.) In this sense, this journey is the only way to show the reality of Christian faith and the way that has been testified through Jesus Christ.

> If in any of your strivings, in any of your actions, in any of your words you truly have had love as your confidant, take comfort, because love abides.[69]

As we travel along this journey, we experience tensions and difficulties each from eternity and the world. The difficulty experienced in the realm of eternity is the need for the sustained determination to hold onto faith as the Word is the foundation for this spiritual journey as we can see in the statement, "faith is the assurance of things hoped for" (Heb 11:1). The commandment that love endures forever is not based on visible evidence but it becomes real as much as we believe the Word. Until that faith becomes a

---

69 Ibid., 300.

reality, we must fight to hold onto faith. It is a fight because the reality of faith is only proved by a path of faith that cannot be turned around.

The reality of eternal love is not separate from the journey of faith. Let me give an example. We can think of walking to the store to buy a gift. We would easily assume walking is a journey and buying a gift at the store is the result. Eternal love, however, is different. This love is shaped only by continually walking the journey of faith and becomes more evident by believing the truth that love abides forever. If we lose our faith in eternal love and stop loving, love stops at the point where there is no faith. In this respect, it is a journey only for those who believe in the ultimate goodness of God, and cannot be stopped as long as we believe that God exists. We will have to stop this journey if we begin to doubt God's existence while walking this journey. The journey to faith is basically based on faith in God's existence.

When despondency at first wants to make you weak, so that you lose the desire to will rightly, in order then in turn to make you strong, alas, as despondency does that, strong in the defiance of forsakenness; when despondency wants to make everything empty for you, to transform all life into a monotonous and meaningless repetition, then you do indeed see all of it, but with such indifference, see the fields and forests becomes green again, see the teeming life in the air and water stirring again, ... and you do indeed know that God is.[70]

The basis of the belief that love abides forever is that God is love and He is eternal. As long as God exists, there is love. Only this faith can enable man to make a leap to God's great demand of love, which will mold mortal man into an eternal being (by restoring him with love). The fact that we can walk this journey only through faith in God means that we will be faced with continuing despair in physical and sensuous realms. In this journey of love, if a person is supported by his senses or his flesh, it will be no longer eternal love. Eternal love makes man leap only to the spirit. The leap to the spirit is possible only by faith. Accordingly, despair in this journey can be

70 Ibid., 300-301.

overcome only by looking at God and turning to hope.

> Naturally no human being is love; he is, if he is in love [*Kjerlighed*], one who loves, Yet love is everywhere present where there is one who loves.[71]

The reality of Christianity embodied by love is as follows: a man goes into the journey of pursuing eternal love by believing in God's presence. To choose true love is like constantly choosing God. Therefore, there is God's presence in those who perform the love of the truth. God's presence is also communicated to others through him because he gives the love of the truth. What is communicated to others is love and God. This is what Kierkegaard said "to love oneself most is to love God, and to love others is to lead him to God."[72] The way in which man loves himself most is to walk on the path of obtaining eternity by loving God, since it is the greatest path, and to lead others to the path of eternity is the way to love others the most.

---

71 Ibid., 301.

72 Ibid., 107.

> Meet all the terrors of the future with this comfort: love abides: meet all the anxiety and listlessness of the present with this comfort: love abides ... what manner of death would be so languishing as would be the case if love did not exist and did not exist eternally![73]

How can we know that the love of the truth is the greatest way of man? It is because of eternity that this love acquires. What does eternity mean for man? It means that man, just a creature, becomes a child of God. If man has no eternity, man is no different from other creatures. Every life except man ends with death. However, man who resembles God's image has the possibility of coming to eternity. From a visible perspective, eternity is the manifestation of God in man by becoming a partaker of the divine nature.[74] Ultimately, this is the very reason man has to believe when embarking on the journey believing that love abides forever. For those who are on this journey, love is neither a gift that has already been obtained at some point in

73 Ibid., 301.

74 2 Pet. 1:4

the past, nor the ultimate gift that will be gained at some point in the future. It is love that is renewed, completed and ever abundant every day.

> It is not an inactive characteristic that love has as such, but a characteristic that acquired at every moment, and also, at every moment it is acquired, is an active work.[75]

Then, does this love not suffer despair? Yes, it does. This great love experiences despair when it is affected by the world that seeks momentary life, when it falls into a lack of faith, and when it gets weary of the continual journey in which the person has to constantly hold unto faith. However, the way to overcome despair is also the belief that love is eternal. Faith encourages us to get out of the wounds of despair and to go on the eternal journey again and to walk with hope, leading us back to the path of acquiring eternity. By faith we remember that God is eternal love. By doing so, we re-establish

---

75 Ibid., 301-302.

our faith on His eternity and have renewed strength supported by His love.

> The one who loves abides, he abides in love, preserves himself in love; what he accomplishes by this is that his love for people abides. He becomes the one who loves by abiding in love; by abiding in love his love abides; it abides, and it is this we now wish to consider.[76]

> If one is truly loving, then one remains that; if one ceases to *be* that, then one never *was* that.[77]

How is the eternal nature of this love delivered to others? One who believes in the love of God devotes himself to obtaining eternity by infinitely giving the life that he earns through faith to others. A person who receives this love will go on the same journey as the one who has delivered the love to him went. In this way, true love along with eternity penetrates through each individual and enters

76 Ibid., 302.

77 Ibid., 303.

into others. If, for any reason, a soul quits this journey by giving up his faith, he is cut off from the love of eternal life and returns to the moment of life. A person who has given love to him will get eternal life by continuously going on this journey, but those who give up belief are cut off from eternal love. In conclusion, eternal life begins in the human soul either through the encounter with Jesus Christ, who is the source of eternal life, or through love that introduces Him. Eventually, eternal life continues by taking the journey on one's own. When he does not continue to walk this great journey, he is cut off from getting eternal life. Therefore, the way to obtain eternal life is to love forever.

Love [*Kjerlighed*] abides—it never wastes away. In spiritual love itself is the spring that flows into an eternal life. That the one who loves also ages over the years and dies in time demonstrates nothing, because his love still remains eternally young. In his love he does not relate himself to temporality, is not dependent upon temporality, as is the relationship in erotic love; eternity is the proper season for his love.[78]

For those who have acquired eternity by true love, giving love will increasingly become the food for soul. In the past when love has tormented him, he has chosen love and re-gained the love of God, while in the moments of despair he has gone forward to the path of hope through the belief that love lasts forever. For him, the stumbling blocks are now removed. Now he has the eternal spring water. He has reached the spring of eternal and true love through love that he has pursued thus far: this is love accomplished by purifying his conscience, by believing everything, by desiring everything, by abandoning his benefits, by covering the sin of others, and by refusing to think of evil. The more he loves, the richer love, eternity, and perfection he gains.

For him, eternity is now the present, not the future. The knowledge of the eternal God becomes a reality to him, and he can enjoy life and believe everything. The outcome of this journey is

78 Ibid., 311.

faith becoming real. This person is the evidence of the reality of God. He has the passion of God, possesses God's will to love, and loves God's patience and compassion with which He saves man by shaping love in man despite all the possibilities of evil. The eternity in him never disappears. That is because it is a gift from God, which he has acquired and earned through his life.

How can a man, a mortal creature, have such great faith? The belief that love endures forever does not exist in this world. It is because it belongs only to God. In spite of the finitude of this world and deception by the misleading natural, selfish senses of man, eternity that God has put in the heart of man reveals itself as the hungry heart. Eventually, a person with a hungry heart finds the hidden spiritual law in which the only way to gain eternal life is by holding onto faith. The endless challenge of man which pushes him toward eternal life that cannot be seen with one's eyes and cannot be proven with reason is the proof that man is indeed created in the image of God and that the human soul is not filled with anything other than God. The fact that God is eternal and that love lasts forever becomes a reality only to those who choose love by faith.

That he who abides never wastes away is certainly an eternal gain for him.[79]

79 Ibid., 313.

Chapter 15

Understanding is the beginning of love

The Lord is merciful and gracious, slow to anger and abounding in steadfast love. He will not always chide, nor will he keep his anger forever. He does not deal with us according to our sins, nor repay us according to our iniquities. For as high as the heavens are above the earth, so great is his steadfast love toward those who fear him; as far as the east is from the west, so far does he remove our transgressions from us. As a father shows compassion to his children, so the Lord shows compassion to those who fear him. For he knows our frame; he remembers that we are dust. (Ps. 103:8-14)

The great thing about Christian love is that it begins with a relationship with God. Christian love begins when God's love overflows to man. Therefore, our journey is love becoming a reality as we materialize our love in others, which is already given as a gift to us through our relationship with God. We start this journey with God. As He is the source of eternal love, we cannot have eternal love apart from Him. What we should remember at the starting point is that God is love but we are not. So we do not know God yet. The only way to have a relationship with God is by faith in love, as the reality of love has yet to come.

For this reason, Christian love begins from the inner being of man. We come to other people as we are connected to God, who is love, by faith. But the love we have to show is imperative love, not preferential love. Obedience to the command of love means that we are not capable of loving others with our own resources. Then, how is the obedience that moves us manifested? The beginning of imperative love is the effort to understand. The fact that man should try to understand others presupposes that man is unable to understand others. It is true. Humans are difficult to understand themselves, but others are even harder to understand. So we have to try to understand. However, a person who does not obey imperative love is unlikely to choose such a difficult endeavor on his own. Understanding is such a difficult task. Understanding others begins with the will to perform the command.

The reality we face when we exert our willingness to understand is our inner self, which either harshly criticizes others or is indifferent to them. However, we must put down our motivation of refusing love, continue our effort to understand, and obey imperative love again. Through this process, the power of this love which moves by centrifugal force, and which will let us know the truth of the world, begins to grow. It is the truth that we will never know when we are in the centripetal force, always heading toward "I". Only when we try to know the truth do we escape from the self-centered world on the basis of our love of truth. The most important truth is that "man does not have love." In other words, "man only loves himself," or "man moves only by motive for himself." Otherwise, it would not be so hard to try to simply understand others without indifference or criticism.

Why is it so difficult to understand others? It is because we do not have compassion for others. The lack of empathy means that there is no room for others in my domain. If you cannot sympathize, you cannot love because love comes from understanding. Obedience to imperative love extends the inner being of the one practicing love before giving any visible fruit of love to others. At least until this point, those who try to love are awakened to the following three facts. First, human beings either love themselves or love for their own sake. Second, human beings do not try to understand others and even give themselves away to ill-advised criticism or indifference. Third, lack of compassion for others is proof that we are locked in our own hell, and the commandment of love is God's salvation plan to bring us out of our own hell. What kind of love can humans do in this hopeless existence? It generally ends in either pity or obsession.

> What is the earnestness of life? ... Earnestness is a person's God-relationship. Whether the thought of God accompanies what a person does, think, and says, earnestness is present; in that there is earnestness.[80]

Why is Christian love so great? It is because the love of God inflates like leaven in the inner being of man who is imprisoned in the hell of the self and finally he gains true freedom when this inside hell is broken. We need to think about how this process takes place. As belief in love comes into our inner self, we turn around from self-conviction to self-skepticism. How is it possible? When we try to understand others, our intellect unravels the inner knowledge we

80 Ibid., 320.

have.

Actually, the knowledge based on which we understand others is knowledge about ourselves. We cannot understand what we do not have knowledge of. We can observe people who are different from us but we cannot understand them. What we have both in our conscious and unconscious is the full potential to understand others. Some may disagree, saying "I have never murdered, then how can I understand a murderer?" However, we cannot make any excuses because the Bible defines one who hates his brother as a murderer (1 Jn. 3:15).

> No, answers eternity, the most important thing is that mercifulness is practiced, or that the help is the help of mercifulness ... From the point of view of eternity, that someone dies is no misfortune, but that mercifulness is not practiced certainly is.[81]

This tells us that we are not incapable of understanding, but we

81 Ibid., 326.

have refused to. Once we accept that we have in us knowledge to understand others, what we should do is to gather knowledge from our inside. The effort to understand others eventually becomes an opportunity to be equipped with genuine self-knowledge. Through efforts to understand our inner world that we did not know before, we become aware of fruits and possibilities of sin in ourselves. As we try to understand and love others more, we will understand and love ourselves more. Loving ourselves referred to here means self-identity.

We generally think that because we love ourselves we put more energy into ourselves, are more generous toward ourselves and tend to be selfish. However, it is not the case. This is often the result of low self-esteem. He who truly loves himself pours himself into the noble value of loving God. To bolster our will to make a leap into eternity, we must acknowledge human existence that does not have any eternal life at all. And to know the true existence of man, he must come out of the prison of self where he is the king, and this only begins when he enters into a relationship of loving others.

A person who recognizes human existence only in others is totally ignorant of oneself. Only those who see their existence through their efforts to understand others are truly honest. He at least realizes that he is not love. Only when he realizes the love of God, which he has received through his efforts to love others, will he who is not love be connected both to others and to God who is eternal. Only then does love become an act of repaying a debt, not a gift.

When another person becomes our true teacher for reflecting ourselves, we will not refuse to love. Even if we would love the vilest sinner in this world, it is just a sinner loving another sinner. Once we know that Christianity is based on the fact that God so loved sinners that He sacrificed His only begotten Son, we cannot refuse to love any sinner because we have been already loved by God as sinners. The effort to understand and sympathize is the first step to obeying the undeniable command of love, only through which can we know the reality of love we have received.

Love is patient and kind; love does not envy or boast; it is not arrogant or rude. It does not insist on its own way; it is not irritable or resentful; it does not rejoice at wrongdoing, but rejoices with the truth. Love bears all things, believes all things, hopes all things, endures all things. Love never ends. As for prophecies, they will pass away; as for tongues, they will cease; as for knowledge, it will pass away. For we know in part and we prophesy in part, but when the perfect comes, the partial will pass away.[82]

Then how is our love manifested in our lives? Outwardly, we will love every moment. By loving, we discover the very love that we have received. Only by loving, we are also connected to eternal life. Only when we try to love, do we find the muscles of love that we previously lacked. In every moment when we choose love, our calm inner world is shaken and those parts of us that are not love emerge to the surface. It means that we will encounter the harsh truth that we are not patient and gentle, that we are jealous, proud, arrogant and rude, that we are not interested in benefiting others and are self-centered, and that we do not rejoice in the truth. We cannot gain eternity unless we conquer our inner being with those muscles of love.

82 1 Cor. 13:4-10

That is now what we wanted to focus attention upon, but rather upon this, that one can be merciful without being able to do the least thing. This is of great importance, since being able to be merciful is certainly a far greater perfection than to be able to do something[83]

Christian love is true and practical love. It is not limited to a great spirit like philanthropy or patriotism. It is love that prioritizes compassion for the poor and helping the needy. In Christian love, we realize the following two facts. First, we are awakened to human existence that we are not love when we make efforts to understand others. Second, we become aware that our continuing efforts to perform imperative love are the only way to transform our inner being into that which is eternal. This love is not hindered by conditions or disturbed by difficulties. This love is a work of sincerity accomplished by a wise man who desires eternity.

83 Ibid., 324.

Eternity understands only mercifulness; therefore if you want to learn to understand mercifulness, you must learn it from eternity.[84]

84 Ibid., 329.

Chapter 16

Fulfillment of love

In my flesh I am filling up what is lacking in Christ's afflictions for the sake of his body (Col 1:24)

Christian love is an act of embodying the truth conveyed by Jesus Christ. Therefore, love comes to us as an imperative task to be completed. Externally the task is a testimony to the truth while internally we gain eternity. The task of infusing eternal life into the truth is what God has entrusted to us. Jesus Himself was the way, the truth, and eternal life. And He showed us the way by setting an example of Himself. We, who believe in Jesus Christ as Savior, begin walking the path of truth by faith, and this faith becomes the priming water to encourage us to love enduringly. This belief signifies that

God is love and that love is eternal. As long as we hold on to that belief, we are constantly choosing love. A person who does not believe in God cannot believe in the ultimate victory of love. Thus, he cannot choose eternal love.

A great invitation to love promises that the God of love will guide and accompany our journey as long as we choose love. Therefore, the more we choose love, the more complete God's presence will be in us. This journey is accomplished in two phases. The first phase is where man, who is not love, fights against distrust, insincerity, and injustice which surface within him through his relationship with others as he continues this journey by believing in the eternal nature of God. So far in this journey, others are not the ultimate beneficiaries of love. It is the heart that desires eternity, which has set off this journey by believing in the presence of love, but human flesh is full of mistrust and unable to believe in the ultimate victory of love.

Therefore, love as a task is a process of overcoming those obstacles by faith. As long as our faith deepens, eternal love dwells in us. As the spirit of man expands into eternity, the Spirit, who dwells in our spirit, can freely use our human flesh as a means of love. This is the war that takes place within us. It is a time when our belief in truth becomes real.

> He was dealing not so much with the unloving person as with himself; he was not fighting to win this battle for the sake of the unloving one but for the sake of the good, and also, in the noble sense, for his own sake.[85]

When we give our heart of believing everything to a person who disbelieves anything, treat a liar with a clean heart, and patiently choose hope for a person who destroys himself, the first thing that comes to our mind is loss and inefficiency. However, when we consider that Christian love is targeted at sinners, not righteous men, and at the sick, not healthy people, we can understand that Christian love is far from efficient. In love, the efficiency of love depends on what our view is.

When we see a person whose love is constantly wasted due to the insincerity of the loved one, a general view is that this love is

85 Ibid., 334.

consumed meaninglessly, assuming that the loved one's insincerity and deceitfulness will eventually insult true love. We can say from a purely human perspective that investment in this love has produced poor results. But faith presents us with a different perspective. Faith views that such investment will continuously raise the purity of love. Then the giver of love becomes the main player of this game. We do not think that the efforts that top-notch artists or athletes make to get the best results is a waste. Rather the many areas they have given up are one of the key factors that contributed to their finest performance.

Likewise what we should focus on when we practice imperative love is not the change of the loved one, but the task of love that we must complete. Maybe God has put the change on hold for the sake of full completion. It is like skipping an appetizer to give the best main dish. If we carry out the task of love from this perspective, we will ultimately gain all: eternal love, eternal life, and God. Jesus' life is a good model. Jesus is the truth and eternal life itself. He proclaimed the truth and loved the children of God, but He was not disappointed in human beings nor did he give up on them.

As Jesus came to die to save man, man's failure to understand or to humiliate Him did not hinder or alter the way of the cross that He had to walk. Whether a mission God has entrusted is accomplished is determined only by God's will and His criteria. If Jesus had assessed His mission based on whether or not man accepted the truth, then Jesus would have neither fulfilled His mission nor loved man. The same is true for the task of love given to us. The first priority in this command is that the inner being of the loved one is fully restored with true love.

His fall is only all too close at hand if he does not permit love and religious consideration to lead him immediately into the next battle, to win the one overcome. When this is done, then the piloting has been correct, past the dangerous reefs where one becomes proud of having persevered in repaying evil with good, where one becomes self-important by having repaid evil with good.[86]

86 Ibid., 337.

When the first phase is completed, we move onto the next level. In this second phase, the loved one is made into fullness with true love. The task of love is not complete without fulfilling these two phases, and it loses eternity at the moment we stop loving. At the first phase, the loved one may bask in love that he received thinking it was a windfall of good fortune or still misunderstanding it. He has yet to understand true love. Meanwhile, the person giving love has passed the first phase and is now united with God. He has no conflict or burden in doing God's will.

The final task of this love is to achieve unity with the loved one as the giver of love had with God. Just as the giver has accomplished the reality of faith by being connected to God only by faith, his counterpart must begin his journey by faithfully following the giver, without knowing the reality of such great love yet. This second journey of achieving unity with man might be more difficult than that with God. We can compare this to a student and a teacher. Until now, the giver has been a hard-working student who did what he had to do on his own. However, from now on, the role of the giver has changed to a teacher who has to teach a slow and clumsy student to reach the same level as his hard-working peers.

In this second journey, we become aware of how great this love is that we have received, which we had never known when we were just receiving it. Until now, we may have likened ourselves to the older brother of the prodigal son, regarding ourselves as hard-working, smart students because we have endeavored to hold on to God, have fought fiercely against unclean spiritual filth within us, and have battled against distrust of the loved one and the evil of the world. But there is one incredible truth that we will never know unless we move to the next step in which we struggle for union with others. It is the difference between God, the Creator and man, the creature. It is the difference between God who created the world from nothing with the Word of life and human beings who were created from dust but given the life of God. Here we come to realize what it meant that God became man or the meaning of the incarnation.

Not many people know how amazing the love of God is. God became flesh to let us know Him, eternal love, and eternal life. Why did God become man? It is explained only by the mercy and love of God. He sent His Son in order to make us His children in the riches of His love. Until the very moment we finally realize this, He has been with us. His abode is the heavenly throne but He came down to this world full of sin and wants to fulfill the love of the truth in us. What God wants us to do is to believe and follow that path.

In the first conflict the battle is against the world for the victory that is won; in the second conflict the battle is with God about that victory. Only when a person in the very moment of victory relinquishes [*afstaa*] the victory to God, only then does a person continue to stand [*bestaa*] after having overcome everything. As long as he was fighting, the opposition in a certain sense helped him to stand [*staa*]; but when he has given God the honor of the victory, God is the support with whose help he continues to stand.[87]

We did not know this difference in the first journey, in which we were made into the love of the truth. We were just fleshly creatures who had barely managed to hold onto the invisible world by faith.

87 Ibid., 333.

Through the accomplishment of the love of the truth in us, God invites us to a small mountain of the truth where He reveals His greatness. When we are restored to the image of God which God created, our eyes are finally open to see God's wonderful creatures and discover God's greatness through the eyes of the Creator. What a wonderful and awesome place of glory!

God presents us with the outcome of this invitation of love and re-sends us down to the valley which is full of neighbors who are to be loved and to be restored. The valley is dark and dim. If no one went down to the valley just like Jesus did, the glory of God would have not been known. At this point, our place changes from the older brother to the prodigal son. We now realize that every journey we took so far has been accomplished by the grace of the Father, and we think we only deserve to be a worker, not His son. The Father, however, has accepted us as His children. Now we become slaves of love. From now on, we will repay the debt of love as His beloved son, not as workers, as He restored us from the prodigal to the beloved son.

As we descend into the valley, we see men who deny eternity, who do not believe anything, and who do not know love. That is exactly what we were before we started this journey. When I tell them to trust me and take my hand, I then come to realize how heartily and sincerely God has persuaded me and tried with all His heart to lead me to the path of eternal life.

God knows how difficult it is for man to believe eternity since man is made of dust, and God also knows how unbelievingly disrespectable that God who is the essential good and love is constantly distrusted by man who is intrinsically neither goodness nor love. God, however, with His love and mercy that is better than life, perseveres with us for a long time and leads us to choose faith. Since we can only know God's heart on that path, God ceaselessly invites us into these works of love.

It is not in the first phase that we realize the love of God when we implant the love of the truth in us, but it is in the second phase when we apply this fulfillment to others. If we stop at the first phase, it does not mean that we have completed the half of the journey but we will fall into a mire. The ultimate culmination is when we make efforts to let this love penetrate into another person.

If we refuse to make such efforts, we will fail to complete the task of love because of our pride and self-satisfaction, which results from our lack of love. What will the works of love achieve? It will obtain God. What we will gain by giving everything is God Himself.

The one who loves hides himself. Lest he disturb, he is, as it were, only covertly present, while that which is really present is the exalted majesty of the good and the true.[88]

88 Ibid., 340-341.

Chapter 17

Love embodies the truth

For whoever would save his life will lose it, but whoever loses his life for my sake will find it. (Matt. 16:25)

Christian love is the only way to embody the truth to which Jesus has testified. The truth becomes visible only by achieving the love of the truth. The reality of the eternal and loving God is revealed in the life of a man who obeys the commandment of love. Thus, man is the only creature who can be a tool to exhibit the reality of the truth.

It is self-denial that discovers that God is.[89]

89 Ibid., 362.

To begin with, we can think of a person who is about to begin the journey to the truth. He has to be a man who loves God, the truth. The truth belongs to God and is not naturally revealed to man. At some point in his life he met the truth and saw its value. Leaping toward the truth signifies man's challenge to gain the Creator and eternity. We can compare this spiritual challenge or transformation to a caterpillar becoming a butterfly.[90]

Just like the final destiny of a caterpillar is a butterfly, the truth tells us that the ultimate destiny of human beings is sons of God, who will take part in the divine nature. Only those who believe the proclamation of this truth can begin their journey to become sons of God. However, we need faith until the end because we cannot believe our identity as sons of God until we take off our cocoon of sins and are led by the Holy Spirit. This is just like a caterpillar

---

90 It is true that a caterpillar becomes a butterfly without any challenge. I used this metaphor to help understand the spiritual conclusion that we cannot grasp easily. A spiritual challenge is different from that of a caterpillar becoming a butterfly in that the former does not take place naturally.

cannot imagine becoming a butterfly until it leaves the cocoon.

> In love of the truth and of humanity to will to make every sacrifice in order to proclaim the truth and, on the other hand, to will not to sacrifice that least bit of the truth.[91]

A person who wants to embody the truth with love is like a caterpillar (natural man) having real faith in a butterfly (son of God). He begins this journey by faith, but ultimately it is a journey that has begun with God. A caterpillar cannot choose a journey of becoming a butterfly on its own because it does not know what a butterfly is. From the moment we hold unto faith, God gives us love for and a thirst for the truth and also a desire to embody the truth. We are often confused because of such desire.

As this journey obviously does not satisfy the fleshly life, human nature becomes an opposing force to deny the new desire. It is impossible to submit ourselves to the task of the command of love

---

91 Ibid., 366.

and also to believe that God's fulfilled law of love is good unless we voluntarily put our opinions and convictions down. However, for a person who has become aware of our hopeless human existence, which is not love, and who knows the need for deliverance from sin, the task of love as the command to embody the truth would be the fascinating greatness to which he is attracted to make a leap.

Those who have fully realized their desperate human existence will set off for the journey to gain love. We, however, still have two temptations at this point. The first is the desire for self-love, which is thoroughly alive and is exerting its influence. The second is the desire to bend the love of the truth to our own satisfaction. We are not totally free from the centripetal force of self-centeredness even though we pursue the truth. As we meet the conditions of true love one by one, the power in the new direction, the love of the truth, gets stronger while the powerful force moving us toward self-centeredness becomes weaker. In this conflict between spiritual and fleshly desires, our power of self-denial has to get stronger in order to embody the truth. In conclusion, the truth is realized only when the self is dead.

God is not seen, and therefore, as God uses this instrument into which a human being has made himself in self-denial.[92]

Christian salvation means a sinner becoming a son of God. It is a recovery to another dimension such as a caterpillar becoming a butterfly. So the challenge for love is the only way to accomplish real salvation. Therefore, we must walk this path as the task to complete. In becoming a butterfly, the most important thing is the caterpillar's self-denial. In order to have an identity as a butterfly, the identity as a caterpillar has to cease. If the caterpillar continues on this journey without hoping for the new identity of a butterfly, it will continually strive to preserve its larval identity. It is an effort not to die as a caterpillar. A butterfly is the new identity it will receive only when it dies as a caterpillar. Death as a caterpillar is the only way to be born again as a butterfly.

God, who has called us as His children, repeatedly reminds us that we are butterflies through the Holy Spirit as we believe and

92 Ibid., 363.

obey Him. As He is the One who knows the reality of a butterfly, God helps us throughout this journey lest we should get weary. Obeying the Holy Spirit who leads us means dying as a caterpillar. If a caterpillar finally becomes a butterfly, it implies the following facts. The caterpillar represents a person who believed in the truth and who has materialized the truth in his life by fulfilling the works of love. Only the embodiment of the truth testifies to the reality of a person's faith. Faith without reality is not faith. How then can man be God's instrument in this journey? The reality of a butterfly is not a gift given from heaven. Man has to surrender to this spiritual desire in his soul to become a butterfly by believing that this caterpillar (representing those who belong to the flesh) will finally become a butterfly (representing those who participate in the divine nature).

Yet only in self-denial can one effectually praise love, because God is love, and only in self-denial can one hold fast to God.[93]

---

93 Ibid., 364.

This desire might bring difficulties and inconveniences to one's existence as the caterpillar (ultimately it means death as the caterpillar). But this person believes that this journey of dying as the caterpillar is a journey to live as a butterfly. Faith leads man to surrender to this spiritual desire. If he falls away from faith at some point and obeys his will to survive as the caterpillar, he may survive as the caterpillar but he has actually killed the life of the butterfly. Thus, self-denial on the part of the caterpillar is not a one-time choice but it has to be determined over and over again until the end of this journey because the fledgling life of the butterfly, which was about to sprout, will stop at that very moment when self-denial is refused on the part of the caterpillar.

In the journey of fulfilling the truth, self-denial is not an option but is rather a prerequisite for obtaining new life. If we do not have hope for eternal life, self-denial will be as painful and hopeless as mental death. Only for those who believe the heavenly existence of flying with wings despite their current hopeless earthly existence of belly crawl and only for those who have thus far sought self-satisfaction locked in their own "jail of self" but now who are willing to participate in the divine nature, will self-denial be an active choice to gain the final glory of God.

True love is self-denial's love. But what is self-denial? It is giving up the moment and the momentary.[94]

This journey of a caterpillar becoming a butterfly implies a journey of the love of the truth in which human beings are shaped into love when they love others. In this journey, true love is validated to us as we give true love to others. What we should remember is the risk of being disoriented by losing our heart to the great value of love and its dynamics. In this journey of acquiring love, the possibility of true love being tainted is not low because human beings are sinners.

The possibility is the temptation to remain in our present life. Since the love of the truth is eternal, we must consume the moment to gain eternity. To give up the present and the moment means to give up self-interest thoroughly and without any selfish motive or

94 Ibid., 369.

interest. This life is exactly the opposite of pursuing self-satisfaction. It is like shaking off any dust left in us in order to complete the love of the truth, which abides forever, to perfection. Such a person is the one who truly loves the truth and who has fulfilled the works of love in order to embody the truth.

In order to be able to praise love, self-denial is required *inwardly* and self-sacrificing unselfishness *outwardly*.[95]

95 Ibid., 374.

Epilogue

When I unexpectedly came across Kierkegaard, I knew that this man would affirm my journey of the truth that I have taken. I had sought the truth and pursued the path that man should walk. I was shocked to find in the Bible that Jesus was the way, the truth, and the life. There are many who pursue the truth and thus, they go after religion, philosophy or ideas. However, I have never seen a person who proclaims that he is the truth. Jesus said that those who seek the truth would come to Him, and as He said, I came closer to him and asked for the life that He promised to give.

It became a motivation for me without any anguish to walk the same path that Jesus had walked. I saw that there was no answer in the numerous paths that people walk, so I chose the narrow road that Jesus introduced. I wondered what would be at the end of this road. It was a hard and lonely walk, but it was a walk with the Holy Spirit and a path full of eternal life. I felt like I was tending a secret garden without any visitors. A thirst for the truth has continuously led me to the way of Jesus. As the Bible says, I was acquiring eternal life in the way of Jesus. In my life, "knowing God and his Son Jesus Christ" (Jn. 17:3) was becoming a reality.

Unexpectedly, I happened to take a Kierkegaard class while I was studying in Canada. The class constantly stimulated my spiritual senses, while other students seemed to be bored and uninterested. The life of Kierkegaard shed light on the way of the truth that I walked. Just in time a lecture on Kierkegaard was opened at the beginning of the next semester. I read his books, and was greatly shocked. Kierkegaard, who I thought was a practical philosopher, was the one who proclaimed the truth, and his proclamation had the power to awaken the human spirit. Most of all, what was most meaningful for me was the fact that he was talking about the way I have walked so far. He explained that the truth of Christianity had to be walked as life and only through the journey would it lead to eternal life.

While walking on this path, I had always wanted to be affirmed about the path because no one could validate this road. However, Kierkegaard was talking as a person who had already walked the path I was walking. Like the name of his book implies, the discovery of Kierkegaard brought "fear and trembling." It was not long before I came to know that Kierkegaard is a person who is hard to understand and is like a star in the sky. The reason for this incomprehensibility is not only because of his ingenuity but also because of his life that had come close to the top of the truth like a star. I believe his words will be understood as much as people understand the truth. I believe that the strong desire to preach the truth as a person who has pursued the truth and walked the way as life is given by God. For that reason, I personally think that the most effective way to introduce the truth in this age is to publicize the writings of Kierkegaard.

For a long time I had *Works of Love* in my mind as the first book of such a series. This book is a voluminous work that has reminded me of the greatness of "love," the value of Christianity, which has become too shallow these days. It also recalled my lifelong journey led by the Holy Spirit. I personally wanted to write a thesis, but God seemed to want me to introduce this topic in my own practical language. This is not a commentary on Kierkegaard's *Works of Love*. My book is basically about the truth that I have come to realize from my life journey.

At first I did not clearly know what to write but soon words flowed out of me. The book contains my personal spiritual journey as well as quotations from *Works of Love*. There are two reason for this. First, I quoted the original text for better understanding because often Kierkegaard's writing is hard to understand, which will make it harder for readers if I do not quote anything but instead try to explain his thoughts with my words. Second, I wrote my life journey as a testimony because the journey of the love of the truth will be the same for everyone if one honestly seeks the truth. I could recognize Kierkegaard because the works of love that he explains is the same path and pattern of loving as mine that was led by the Holy Spirit.

I hope that readers will discover the greatness of love and venture into the challenge of loving Christianly. Since we do not wish to gain eternity, we stay in the love of self-satisfaction focusing on the moment. Eternity is the life in which the Creator comes into and dwells in the creature. It is the Creator's salvation plan and a task that must be done by man's obedience. What is salvation? What is the reality of faith? It is the embodiment of the love of the truth in the life of the creature. I do not doubt that those who accept the great challenge as the invitation from the Creator will be blessed.

Challenge yourself with this amazing task of love to achieve eternity and God, and to embody the truth!

How rarely does the eternal get so much control over a person that love in that person begins to establish itself eternally or to form the heart. Yet this is the essential condition for bearing love's *own* fruit by which it is known.[96]

---

96 Ibid., 12-13.

HISWAY

Love Embodies the Truth

Published in 2019 by HISWAY

HISWAY website (For purchasing): https://hiswayglobal.modoo.at

Ha, Munjung
Love Embodies the Truth / by Munjung Ha;
edited by Jayong Kim / Roger and Janet Samra
Translation of: Sarangeun Jillireul Guhyeonhanda

ISBN 979-11-956615-3-4

For more information, please email us at hiswaypublishing@naver.com.
Printed and bound in the Republic of Korea
First Edition